Watery Grave

to die is to live

Kyle W. Bauer

Foreword by Joy Dawson

Watery Grave

Unless otherwise noted, all Scripture quotations are taken from The Holy Bible New King James Version (NKJV), Copyright © 1982 Thomas Nelson, Inc.

ISBN 978-0-578-18551-4

Cover photo from www.unsplash.com

Dedicated to my wife Teresa who is an amazing woman of God without whom ministry would hardly be possible.

¡Te amo!

Also, a special thanks to Bonnie Willey and Jackie Murillo who spent many hours reading and re-reading this book.

CONTENTS

Foreword   i

Introduction   1

1   Baptism   5
2   Baptism is Freedom   15
3   Baptism: The Watery Grave of Death   27
4   Baptism: The Waters of Resurrection   38
5   Baptism: Preparation, Purification, and Participation   61
6   Baptism: Entrance into God's Family   80
7   The Baptism of Jesus   94
8   Baptism: Open Doors to the Supernatural   115

Addendum: Infant Baptism   133
Appendix   135
About the Author   139

Foreword

My dear friend Kyle Bauer has given us a vital package of life changing truths that come from the most reliable and life changing source, the Word of God.

Kyle writes with strong convictions and a real sense of authority. This comes from the genuiness of his living out these truths of the three baptisms and their implications in his own daily life. He's the real deal.

I have known Kyle since he was a boy and two things have always characterized him. He was never in a conformative mold to his environment, therefore never had a chance to become "moldy." He was always all or nothing at all. He had great appeal to me!

Over many years I have followed his life closely, loved him dearly and always believed he would become the genuine, vital man of God and spiritual leader that he is today.

I highly recommend the well researched, well presented, timeless truths in this book. It would make a great resource for teaching new believers in Christ, as well as challenging and instructing those who are not so new, to be more conformed to the image of the Lord Jesus.

Joy Dawson
International Bible teacher, Missionary, and Author

Watery Grave

Introduction

No one likes a story that ends badly. No one likes it
when the hero dies. We don't like the sense of loss,
hopelessness, or the victory of the villain prevailing
over good. Shakespeare's famous play, Romeo and
Juliet, has a horrible ending. We root for the success of
the forbidden lovers while wanting love to triumph
over bitter hatred—but the lovers (spoiler alert) die,
and the story ends in catastrophe. The hatred between
the families of the two lovers is allowed to persist, and
the only two people who were able to see beyond the
hate are dead. We don't like stories like this because we
know life ought to be different, and we desperately
hope that it will be.

When we read a book or watch a movie and there is an
unexpected twist in the story where everything that was
good and right experiences a sudden catastrophe, we
often times feel a punch in the gut as if we are living the
same catastrophic loss of goodness along with the
protagonist. Most stories, however, do not end badly,
and ours certainly does not either. Yet, catastrophe
strikes in the midst of our story, too.

God created everything to be good as He is good, and
He then topped it off with the crown of His creation,
humanity, to be as He is. Then catastrophe struck—

humanity lost all of the goodness given by God due to satan's deceptive promise that we could have more power and knowledge for ourselves if only we would loose the restrictive fetters of the Almighty. Humanity bought the lie hook, line, and sinker. The serpent's promise was as empty as it was destructive. As a result, the catastrophic loss humanity suffered is the most heartbreaking in all of literature. It may not seem so heartbreaking or emotionally wrenching in reading Genesis 1-3, but when we realize that this is much more than a literary catastrophe, but it is *our* real-life catastrophe and the loss we suffer is that of our own lives and of God's eternal presence, suddenly the disaster becomes more real. This is not a fairytale or an ancient legend. Nor is this one of those horrible dreams that seems so real. No. This is true.

The word "catastrophe" is of Greek origin and is a compound word made of "cata," (meaning "down/against") and "strophe" (meaning "twist/turning about"). Thus, a catastrophe is a sudden, disastrous turn of events. So often in literature, part of what brings the gut-wrenching disaster upon the hero is an imposition of an impossible decision or doing what no one else can or will do in the midst of almost impossible circumstances. Often times the noble hero sacrifices himself or herself for the good of others or fights heroically against the most daunting odds—and seems to fail. Life was given in vain, and all efforts have been for naught.

Each of us is in the middle of our story. The catastrophe has already struck and the life we live is bereft of the goodness that God intended for us. We are in the precarious life-or-death position even now, and God is looking to turn it around. He is asking us to make the ultimate sacrifice—to give Him our lives. He is asking for everything, and it seems that we will get little in return. God asks us to follow Him into the waters of baptism, to sink down and drown in the depths of a watery grave and lose everything we have ever known...and for what? For His sake? Seems like a raw deal. It seems like God is compounding the catastrophe.

Compounded catastrophe is not part of the great stories that we love to read, hear, and watch over and over again—these rarely end in catastrophe. After the sudden, disastrous downturn of events, there then comes a "eucatastrophe." "Eu" comes from the Greek for "good" and this word, coined by J.R.R. Tolkien, is a favorable turn of events that few saw coming, but ensures the ultimate triumph of good. In Tolkien's series <u>The Lord of the Rings</u>, good defeats evil, in which evil, having overwhelming odds, is swallowed up in sudden destruction. Good triumphs. In the Bible, Jesus, who is the long-awaited Messiah, the miracle worker, the compassionate forgiver of sins, and the hope of Israel, is brutally put to death. As all of His followers mourn not only His death but the death of all their hopes and dreams, Jesus suddenly rises from the dead in an eucatastrophe and fulfills the centuries-old prophecies and promises of God.

It is in catastrophe that God works the greatest
eucatastrophes. The destruction of God's goodness in
humanity is only recovered through catastrophic
death—Jesus' death and, therefore, our death along
with Him. Our symbolic death is required of us in
baptism—the watery grave. Our death entails
everything of the catastrophic life that we have lived up
to this point. Though the death is symbolic, it feels very
real. We are being asked by God to abandon everything
for His sake. Allow our hopes, dreams, ambitions,
biases, ways of thinking, and ways of living to forever
be drowned in the water. Yet, it is in this catastrophic
death that God is able to suddenly turn everything in
our favor. All that was lost from the beginning is
changed in an instant!

As you move through this book, you will see that our
death in this watery grave is actually a symbolic
passage into the fullness of life that is available to us in
Jesus Christ. Jesus said that he who loves his life will
lose it, but he who loses his life for My sake will find it
(Matthew 10:39). There can be no resurrection without
there first being death. The only way to truly live in the
transforming, supernatural life in God's Kingdom is to
pass through the watery grave.

I
𝕭aptism

This book is for you! It is for you if you are interested in being baptized, are about to be baptized, or if you have already been baptized. As we will see throughout this book, water baptism is a representation of the salvation—the *full* salvation—that Jesus worked for us. Salvation is more than being forgiven of sin—though it is the essential component! You will see that baptism is also a much larger concept than the simple ritual of immersion in water. Jesus commanded us in Matthew 28:19 to be baptized in the Name of the Father, the Son, and the Holy Spirit. In other words, there are different components to the idea of baptism that give us a much deeper understanding of it.

Baptism itself is more than simply the pronunciation of a pastor putting you under the water as he or she pronounces, "I baptize you in the name of the Father, the Son, and the Holy Spirit." Baptism fully symbolizes the way that God the Father brings us into His family and we inherit all the spiritual blessings of His Kingdom, the way that God the Son has saved and delivered us from our slavery to sin, and the way God the Holy Spirit gives us supernatural power to do the same works Jesus did in order to minister God's life to a broken world. Baptism is the symbol of our salvation—our **_entire_** salvation.

Salvation is much more than a singular point in time. It is instantaneous when we repent of our sins and confess Jesus Christ as our Lord and Savior. But it is also the complete process of God in Jesus Christ for the **restoration** of humankind to relationship with Him, the **renewal** of physical, emotional, and spiritual health, the **recovery** of destiny all were created for, and the **refilling** with power to fulfill that destiny.

Yes, this book is for you! I want to invite you to walk through this book with an open heart and allow God to open up to you, not just the rite of baptism, but the way to walk in its fullest power and efficacy for your life today.

Baptism's Doorway

As we launch into this study of the meaning of water baptism, it is important that we go in with the proper mindset as to what God always intended it to be. Baptism is more than a rite or ritual that Jesus Christ established. God did not establish baptism in order for His children to earn points or be positioned to more effectively vie for His affections, or advance our spiritual status. Nor is baptism given to elevate ourselves over others who have not yet taken this step of faith. Rather, Jesus came to establish a way of living in which we are to follow Him so that ***His life*** might be ***our life***; ***His power*** might be ***our power***; and ***His victory*** might be ***our victory***.

Water baptism is the symbol of our living, growing salvation in which we become part of a new family and learn to live in a new Kingdom. Our salvation is also intended to be a point of entry into a much larger life— a life of becoming the people God intended us to be. All this means is simply this: A new everything requires a new way of living—and we have much to learn!

Before beginning His public ministry, before working any miracles, preaching any sermons, resurrecting the dead, healing the sick or casting out demons, Jesus was first baptized to *"fulfill all righteousness"* (Matthew 3:15). In order to understand why Jesus was baptized and why we are commanded to follow Him into the waters, we need to look beyond the ritual of simply going under the water.

Baptism is not a rite that makes us part of a religious institution; rather it unites us to the very life Christ Jesus exemplified for us and ushers us into a supernatural way of living beyond our sin and a life full of the Spirit of God. The mandate for baptism that Jesus gave us releases the life, freedom, and power in our lives, and this power is to be effectuated and

7

remain in force during our whole life. This life of salvation goes far beyond one solitary experience. The act of baptism is much more than simply getting wet. Baptism is not for salvation, but it is the representation of the reality of the continual power for life transformation provided to us in our salvation. When we are immersed in the waters of baptism and welcome this new, supernatural way of living, it is in essence, the gateway into the process of learning to live and growing as a disciple of Jesus Christ.

Perhaps you may be asking the question, "If it is only a symbol or a representation, then why do we need to do it at all?" For one, it is a step of obedience—Jesus told us to do this (Matthew 28:19). In all my years of knowing Jesus, I have found that simple steps of obedience open up doors to the spiritual realm and release the flow of God's blessing upon our lives. In fact, in my years of pastoring, I have witnessed four steps of obedience—four fountains which flow from our being—that have never failed to release God's blessings in one's personal life: 1) Water Baptism as a symbol of our salvation, 2) Tithing and giving offerings, 3) The words of the mouth, and 4) Sexual purity. These are actions that align our lives with God's established ways of living and are the fountains that flow out of our lives to the world around us (ie. The flow of our spiritual life, our money, our words, and our procreation/identity). When we submit these things to the Lord and live in obedience to the way He has designed life to be lived as revealed through His Word, these fountains of life flow with the power and blessing of God and are kept from become polluted and diseased fountains which disallow for a healthy life. God asks us to act on His Word in a small way, and through that action God does a big thing! Great power is unleashed in the physical expression of a spiritual reality. Much like a wedding is a physical symbol of the reality of two lives uniting, baptism is a physical symbol of the reality of us uniting to Jesus Christ.

We cannot live into the full reality of God's promised blessing and power if we have not first submitted to this directive from the Lord. Baptism has to do with the submission of every part of our lives to the Lordship of Jesus Christ. I have known people who love God, are very sincere in their faith, and have followed Jesus for many years without having been baptized. However, the moment they decided to get baptized, there was an immediate advance in their relationship with God along with freedom in areas of their lives where they had struggled before. Likewise, I have seen people who begin to tithe and couples who decide to marry begin to live in freedom and blessing that was not possible before. We never lose when we decide to live in obedience to what God asks of us. The Creator of life knows very well how it ought to be lived, and we are blessed when we live it the way it was designed by God.

WELLS OF LIVING WATER
The truth of baptism goes far deeper than the physical water we enter, and the power of baptism goes beyond

the moment of immersion. Baptism introduces us to a lifestyle of walking in God's freedom and power. Baptism is an act of faith, and faith is what enacts baptism's power. If sincerity, faith, and truth do not accompany a person getting in the water and the experience is treated as nothing more than a ritual, then the reality and power of all baptism is meant to symbolize is stymied. If it is nothing more than a ritual done to somehow please other people and not done with sincerity of heart before God, at the end of the ceremony, all you have is a wet person, not a transformed person! Living out the power of baptism requires **continued diligence on our part**, and we in turn encounter the **continued stream of grace on God's part** toward us.

Our diligence does not activate God's grace and goodness as if we could gain it through enough good works. Rather, God freely gives His grace to those who come in simple, child-like faith. But as it would with a diligent student in his academic studies, such diligence allows us to pursue, understand, live out, and discover more of the living realities God has already applied to our lives through Jesus Christ. The promise of Jesus to us is that *"everyone who asks receives, and he who seeks finds,"* (Matthew 7:8). Furthermore, Jesus said *"with the same measure you use, it will be measured to you; and to those who hear, more will be given,"* (Mark 4:24). Diligence in faith and pursuit of God is rewarded with deeper, growing, and more substantive relationship with Him, (Hebrews 11:6).

Jesus declares that *"He who believes in Me, as the Scripture has said, out of his heart will flow rivers of living water."* The Apostle John, in the next verse goes on to explain Jesus' declaration: *"But this He spoke concerning the Spirit, whom those believing in Him would receive; for the Holy Spirit was not yet given, because Jesus was not yet glorified"* (John 7:38-39). The water Jesus was talking about is the continual flowing of the Holy Spirit in and through our lives. What a wonderful picture of baptism! As we submit to the Lord in the waters of baptism, we are allowing the work of the Holy Spirit to well up in us, around us, and through us.

Water is one of the quintessential images in Scripture of the work of God's Holy Spirit. It is necessary for God's people to constantly live in the vital, streaming river of God's grace—grace that does not come from ourselves but grace that springs up from within us by the supernatural work of the Holy Spirit that keeps us growing and strong. The power of God released to us in baptism is meant to keep us advancing in God's purposes during our entire lives. As we will see throughout this book, the waters of baptism are for freedom, purification, new life, access to God's promises, growing in God's family, and power for living the way God desires.

When Jesus spoke to the Samaritan woman at the well, He said, *"but whoever drinks of the water that I will give him will never be thirsty again. The water that I will give him will become in him a spring of water welling up to eternal life"* (John 4:14). The image of Jesus giving living water that becomes a life-giving well inside us is a beautiful picture of what God releases in us through baptism. The Lord, with our participation, digs a well in our hearts that goes deeper than the shallowness of our own human efforts to fulfill the thirst within us. The deeper the well goes, the greater the blessing of God's grace to flow to and satisfy the deepest longing of our soul. The obedience of baptism provides for a continual flow of God's grace to us.

In Genesis 26, we see the result of the union between God's grace and our diligence in the story of Isaac. Isaac, the son of Abraham, was living in the land of the Philistines. The Lord had blessed and multiplied him as He had done with his father. He was so blessed by God that the Philistines became jealous and stopped up the wells of water that Abraham had dug.

Wells give water, and water represents life to all living things, but it was especially important to a man whose livelihood was in livestock and farming. Blocking off the flow of God's blessings and provision was the Philistines attempt to run Isaac out of the region. Similarly, Satan will make every attempt possible to muddy, clog, and hinder every good thing that God is doing in us. Just as the Philistines threw anything into the wells that would choke its life-giving flow, satan will try and block up our lives with the sin and temptation of this world to stop the flood of God's grace and power to us. Isaac, however, would not allow such things to rule his life, nor would he allow the blessings of God's promises to be stolen from him. Not only did Isaac re-dig the wells of his father, he went out and dug four more—even in dry desert! (Genesis 26:17-32).

Even though the wells of Abraham were stopped up, the fact is that everywhere Isaac went, he dug wells, and everywhere he dug he found water. Even in the midst of difficult circumstances and dry deserts, he dug until he found water. Wherever we go and in whatever we do, when we decide to be people who live out the high calling of God in the power of His baptism, Satan will seek to oppose us at every point. Just as Isaac found water, wherever we go, wherever God places us, and in whatever we do, we, too, will find the wells of His grace filling our souls as we live in the power of God's Spirit in baptism's reality.

His grace, abundance, power, and Spirit—the very life of Jesus Christ into which we have been baptized—are enough to sustain us in the midst of the difficulties that life brings our way. We are not to give up or give in, but to continue walking in faith and perseverance as Jesus' disciples. As with an ever-flowing well of water, there is enough of God's heavenly resources to draw on at every moment of life and in every state of our souls. As we continue diligently digging, searching, and looking for more of Him, even in the midst of life's most difficult circumstances, we will find that God's well never runs dry.

The Bible gives us even more insight into the wells of salvation that are being dug in our lives. In John 4, Jesus speaks to the Samaritan woman of "wells of living water" He provides which will satisfy the deep thirst of the human heart. Later, in John 7:37-38, Jesus says, *"If anyone thirsts, let him come to Me and drink. He who believes in Me, as the Scripture has said, out of his heart will flow rivers of living water."* The water that we find in coming to the Savior is both a **well** and a **river**. Through the work of His Spirit in us, and in our submission to Him in baptism, we allow Him to open up new wells in us from which we may draw more and more of His living water. The wells of water fill our souls and then overflow out of us to become the rivers of the living water of the Holy Spirit that overflow out of us to revive the dry, thirsty world around us.

II

Baptism is Freedom

The concept of baptism did not begin with
Jesus or with John the Baptist. Though the
Apostle Peter briefly mentions the Flood as a
baptism for the cleansing of the conscience, the
understanding of baptism really begins with
Israel's freedom from Egypt and the colossal
miracle of the crossing of the Red Sea. The
psalmist references this miracle in Psalm 98:1-
3:

*Oh sing to the LORD a new song, for He
has done marvelous things! His right
hand and His holy arm have worked
salvation for Him. The LORD has made
known his salvation; He has revealed
His righteousness in the sight of the
nations. He has remembered His
steadfast love and faithfulness to the
house of Israel. All the ends of the earth
have seen the salvation of our God.*

(ESV)

Although we do not know who composed this psalm, we do know that he was Hebrew—an Israelite. The psalmist is singing of the salvation of God and the wonders He did for His people Israel. In the Hebrew mentality, the salvation of God and His "marvelous things" are a reference to the moment when God rescued His people from slavery in Egypt and then opened up the Red Sea to make a way of escape and freedom for them.

This psalm declares that it is by God's mercy— his *hesed*—that God saved His people. Today, we experience this same mercy through His marvelous work of salvation in Jesus Christ. The Hebrew word *hesed* refers to God's constant, faithful, and unconditional love and mercy that He has toward all people. It is **because** of the greatness of His faithfulness, love, and mercy (*hesed*) to people that God does what He does for us.

It is interesting to note that in these three verses, the word salvation is mentioned three times. God worked His salvation in Israel by freeing them from slavery in Egypt. After they made their Exodus from the land of their captivity, their freedom was finalized through God's marvelous works of opening up a way toward a new life of freedom through the waters of the Red Sea.

In Hebrew, *yasha* is the root word for the various forms of the word *salvation*. The name *Yeshua*, which is the Hebrew name for Jesus, is derrived from the same root as *yasha*. In fact, verse three of Psalm 98 literally says, *"All the ends of the earth have seen the YESHUA* [salvation] *of our God!"* In Jesus, God works His salvation for us. Jesus Christ is the greatest way God could possibly show His faithful love and mercy *[hesed]* because it is through Jesus that we can be reconciled again to God. It is in Jesus that we have salvation—and it is following Him into the waters of baptism that we begin to literally act out the salvation story of being freed from our sins.

Freedom from Sin

As we read the story of Israel and what God did for His people, we come to realize that their story is ours, too. For more than 400 years Israel had been captive and enslaved in Egypt. Their oppression was long and cruel, but God had compassion on them and set Himself to free them. In the same way Israel suffered slavery in Egypt, we are slaves to sin (Romans 6:17). Sin, like the Egyptians had been, is a cruel master. It

is the cruelty of violence which people
have suffered, the cruelty of betrayals
and hurts by loved ones, the cruelty of
depression, that, like a slave-driver,
pushes us toward addictions, and the
cruelty of lies, hatred, and every other
thing that suffocates life instead of
allowing it to thrive. Sin is a cruel
master and there is no way we can
escape its bondage on our own. But, as
with Israel, God saw our desperate
circumstances, and it moved Him with
such compassion, He sent a Deliverer to
free us from sins' punishing, cruel grip
on our lives.

On the night God freed His people from slavery
in Egypt, He told the Israelites that they were to
take a one-year-old lamb, kill it, and put its
blood over the door of their houses. This would
save them from the plague of death that was
about to be unleashed over Egypt. This is the
night that is known as the Passover—when
death "passed over them" because of the blood
of the lamb. Without that blood, they, too,
would have succumbed to the pestilence of
death.

The first Passover was a shadow—a symbol—for
the real Passover that was accomplished in
Jesus Christ. As in the first Passover, there is

the pestilence of death that is over every human being because of sin. But Jesus is the Lamb that God sent to us. In John 1:29, John the Baptist declares, *"Behold, the Lamb of God who takes away the sin of the world!"* Jesus paid for our sins and won our freedom through His death on the Cross. Because of His spilled blood on that Cross, the death sentence, that we had because of our sins, "passed us over" (See Romans 6:23).

Israel's salvation was secured that night, but the story is not over yet. The very next day, Pharaoh, the king of Egypt who had lost his firstborn son during the plague of death, was so disconsolate that he finally allowed the Israelite slaves to leave Egypt. With great joy and a great exodus, the Israelites left 430 years of slavery behind them and followed Moses toward their freedom into the promises of God. A few short days later, they found themselves camping at the shores of the Red Sea:

Now it was told the king of Egypt that the people had fled, and the heart of Pharaoh and his servants was turned against the people; and they said, "Why have we done this, that we have let Israel go from serving us?" So he made ready his chariot and took his people with him. Also, he took six hundred

choice chariots, and all the chariots of
Egypt with captains over every one of
them. And the Lord hardened the heart
of Pharaoh king of Egypt, and he
pursued the children of Israel; and the
children of Israel went out with
boldness. So the Egyptians pursued
them, all the horses and chariots of
Pharaoh, his horsemen and his army,
and overtook them camping by the sea
beside Pi Hahiroth, before Baal
Zephon. (Exodus 14:5-9)

Mountains blockaded one side, the sea created
a barrier on another, and desert closed in on
the third. The Israelites had nowhere to run
with Pharaoh and his armies bearing down on
the newly-freed slaves. It was there that God
worked His most wonderful miracle and
brought complete freedom to His people by
opening up a way in the midst of the sea. God
made a way where one did not exist before. The
Egyptians pursued Israel through the sea, but
as the Egyptians were in the middle and the
Israelites safely on the other side, God closed
the waters over them. What Moses had told the
Israelites came true:

"Do not be afraid. Stand still, and see the
salvation of the Lord, which He will
accomplish for you today. For the Egyptians

*whom you see today, you shall see again no
more forever. The Lord will fight for you, and
you shall hold your peace"* (Exodus 14:13-14).

There is no barrier in our lives that cannot be
broken by the power of God!

In the same way, when the power of the blood
of Jesus frees us from sin's slavery, we are
assured total and complete freedom from its
death-grip. The death and resurrection of Jesus
Christ assures our salvation. Only in Jesus is
there power for salvation and an "exodus" from
our sins. In fact, Jesus used the term "exodus"
to describe His death on the cross in Luke 9:31
(*the word "departure" in the Greek is "exodon"
literally "exodus"*). There is amazing
significance in Jesus' allusion to the cross and
the Exodus story. ***The death of Jesus is a
new Exodus for all who believe in Him.***

However, just as in the first Exodus story, satan
does not want to lose the slaves taken from
him. Even after our salvation, our sins come
running after us to again enslave us and take us
back into captivity. Addictions, memories, ways
of thinking, habits, and all the things that we
did as slaves to sin, lie waiting to trap us again.
The temptations are enormous, and at times it
seems that the salvation we first rejoiced in is
now somehow ineffective in the face of our past

that tries to sweep us away.

When the Israelites saw Pharaoh and his armies racing after them, they began to accuse God of wanting to kill them by saying to Moses:

Because there were no graves in Egypt, have you taken us away to die in the wilderness? Why have you so dealt with us, to bring us up out of Egypt? Is this not the word that we told you in Egypt, saying, "Let us alone that we may serve the Egyptians"? For it would have been better for us to serve the Egyptians than that we should die in the wilderness. (Exodus 14:11-12).

We have the tendency to blame God or to not believe Him when the darkness of our past threatens to overwhelm us. But the reality is that God has a miracle waiting for us!

1 Corinthians 10:2 says, *"all were baptized into Moses in the cloud and in the sea."* The march through the Red Sea is one of the keys to understanding the power of baptism. After coming to Christ in repentance for salvation, God wants to break and remove every last trace of the sin of our past. Baptism is a new beginning and total liberation from the chains that had us bound to the cruel master of sin.

Baptism is the activation of the freeing power of the Savior in our lives right here and right now.

New Life

I met Liz at a restaurant. I was there by myself with my Bible, and she, with her husband and friends, were at the table right next to me. I was simply eating my meal and minding my own business when she unexpectedly plopped down right in front of me and asked very intensely if I was a Christian. I was somewhat startled and told her I was a Christian pastor. "Good," she said, "I have a lot of questions."

For the next hour we talked about her very pain-filled life and about how Jesus is the redeemer and restorer of our lives. After a while she prayed to ask Jesus to be her Lord and Savior, and both she and her husband showed up at church the following day for Sunday service full of joy and thankfulness for her new found love for Jesus. Later that week, she and her husband sat down with my wife and me, where for three hours, she told us the most horrific, gut-wrenching, painful life story that I have ever heard in all my years as a pastor. More than once we were moved to tears as she told her story of betrayal, demonic assaults, an abusive mother, bad decisions, violence, a loveless marriage, broken family relationships, and way too much death. We met with her and her husband on several occasions during the following weeks and guided them in their first steps in their new life in Jesus. All I can say is that I have never seen such an amazing life transformation is such a short period of time. Jesus got a hold of Liz's heart BIG TIME!

Very soon after receiving Jesus, Liz told me she wanted to be baptized. We talked about the meaning of baptism and we set a date. Her baptism was amazing, and I had the honor and privilege of doing it. The presence of God met her in the waters—and even some of her family travelled from out of state to witness it! Almost as soon as she had been baptized, suddenly she and her husband had to move to another city. I had only known Liz for about eight weeks. A few weeks after the baptism she texted me and I want to share some of what she said:

Hello, Kyle and Teresa! I just wanted to share how amazing life is!!! Jesus has not only blessed me with a house, He has given me a home with an entire family!!! I had a talk with my mom...she could not believe how wrong she was...she began to cry saying please forgive me...I'm so happy I have my mom back!...and most of all my husband and I are the best of friends, we're working together as a team and putting Jesus first before anything!...The day I was baptized...I felt like the day I came out of prison, like if I was locked up in a box or something. Like I broke out of something that was holding me back away from happiness! Now I feel free from bondage...My husband noticed a great difference in me as well as my children and family...I'm sooooo happy to walk with a huge smile on my face every day because every day is special because God allowed it!

God is inviting us into the waters of baptism. Neither the water itself nor the church baptistery are anything special or extraordinary. ***The water is a physical representation of the spiritual reality of God's working in our lives.*** There is amazing power to release us from bondage and bring in a flow of God's restorative power as we physically walk through the waters of baptism. But even after baptism, God's delivering power is in effect so that we continue to live in the freedom He provides. God wants to advance our lives and break every power and vestige of control that sin once had over us. Even if there are times we feel the past is closing in on us, the words of Moses still ring true for our life in Jesus today, *"Do not be afraid. Stand still, and see the salvation of the Lord, which He will accomplish for you today. For the Egyptians whom you see today, you shall see again no* *more forever. The Lord will fight for you!"* The slave-master of your past and your sins will be forever drowned in the watery grave of baptism.

II

Baptism

The Watery Grave of Death

Symbols are powerful representations of deep truths and spiritual realities. My wife and I wear wedding rings on our hands as an outward symbol of a deep covenant union. Something as simple as a Christmas tree is symbolic of Jesus who was born to be our everlasting life just as the tree is an "Evergreen", and that He is the Light of the world as we decorate it with lights. This tree also reminds us that Jesus was born to die "on a tree" (Galatians 3:13) for our salvation. The symbol of the Cross is a powerful sign that points to Jesus' delivering work in His death and resurrection. As followers of Jesus, symbols serve to unite humanity to the purposes of God.

Think of it this way: Romans 12:1 tells us that

we are to offer ourselves as a living sacrifice to the Lord. A living sacrifice requires physical expression. Baptism is a physical response to a spiritual reality. The reality is that we are participating with Jesus in His death and resurrection, and the response that is required of us is the physical baptism.

A symbol is powerful, but it has no power in and of itself—it is a shadow. Saint Augustine, the great Christian theologian of the 4th and 5th centuries, wrote about the sacraments of Baptism and Communion as *"visible signs of an invisible grace."*[1] A shadow exists because there is something real blocking the light and, thus, is casting a shadow. Baptism is the shadow of the reality of what God is doing in us. Our faith in God and our salvation revolve around two things: the death and resurrection of Jesus Christ, and baptism shadows these two events. St. Augustine goes on to say, *"The water, therefore, manifesting exteriorly the sacrament of grace, and the Spirit effecting interiorly the benefit of grace, both regenerate in one Christ that man who was generated in Adam."*[2] In other words, there is a spiritual reality that will not be fully activated in our lives if we will not physically respond in this manner.

In the Gospel of Luke, Jesus refers to the Cross

as both an **exodus** and a **baptism**, (Luke 9:31; 12:50). Baptism is, in its essence, a death. It is the baptism of His death in which we are participating when we are submerged beneath the water. When Jesus died on the Cross, He bore all the sins of all the world—yours and mine, too! In order for us to be saved from the death that our sin produces, a price must be paid: *"For the wages of sin is death but the gift of God is eternal life in Christ Jesus our Lord"* (Romans 6:23). It was the price of my death— and your death—that Jesus paid on the Cross. The Cross is the testimony of the immensely high price of sin. In the waters, we are *"baptized into Christ Jesus,"* and *"baptized into His death,"* (Romans 6:3).

Jesus teaches in Matthew 16:25, *"For whoever desires to save his life will lose it, but whoever loses his life for My sake will find it."* Every person desires to save his or her life...but lose it? The great dichotomy of our faith is that only through the loss of our lives can we find them again in Christ. Saving our lives only happens through death. In Jesus' death we are united to Him (Romans 6:5). The Apostle Paul also asserts in Galatians 2:20, *"I have been crucified with Christ; it is no longer I who live, but Christ lives in me..."* Death to sin must occur in order to enable us to have relationship with God because it is sin that separated us from

Him in the first place!

Jesus Christ is completely human and completely God. He died and rose again as both God and human. God united Himself to humanity when He stepped into our world as one of us at His birth. As a human being—part of the human race—He is united to our destiny of sin and death. Yet, unlike you and me, He lived with no sin. The unfathomable miracle of Jesus as God-in-flesh, and flesh-in-God, is what made Him able to win back humanity from sin's captivity. Being human, Jesus' death satisfied sin's death penalty over the human race; being divine, His sacrifice was satisfactory for the entirety of humankind. ***Just as God united Himself to humanity in Christ Jesus, as the perfect human, Jesus was able to unite humanity back to God.***

Union with God is obtained through Jesus' death and resurrection. Since His death satisfied our death, we can live again with Him. In this new union with God, baptism could also be identified as a type of wedding. When God created us, He did it so that we could be together and to share life together. Creation can be understood to be much like a wedding with God creating us for the purpose of being with us and us with Him. However, the introduction of sin into humanity acted like a divorce in that

sin completely broke our union with the
Creator. But God was not done with the human
race. Instead of walking away from us, He
sought a way to restore the broken relationship.

God, through Israel, established a covenant
people for Himself to whom He would be
bound and once again share life with humanity.
It would be through this people that the rest of
the nations of the world would know God. But
yet again, separation prevailed due to Israel's
persistent infidelity and idolatry. In Jeremiah
3:8, God, in speaking to His covenant people,
directs His comments to them as His wife:

*"Then I saw that for all the causes for which
backsliding Israel had committed adultery, I
had put her away and given her a certificate of
divorce..."*

The Apostle Paul explains in Romans 7:1-3 that
marriage is for life, and only when the partner
dies is the spouse free to marry again. Though
God had issued a divorce to His unfaithful
people, He also died, thus freeing Himself from
the old covenant and able to marry His people
again in a new covenant! We are united to
Christ in His death and resurrection, and we
are *in Christ* and *"Christ lives in [us]."*

We can be united again to God in this covenant

relationship. We are dead to all the dirtiness of sin so that we can live to God again. Jesus' death *was our death*. One theologian explains our death with Jesus saying: *"Note that Paul did not write, 'we were buried **like** Him,' but 'buried **with** him.' That is, we were laid with him in his grave in Jerusalem! So, too, the death he died on the cross was our death also."*[3] Paul also details our participation in the death of Jesus in Romans 6:11-14:

Likewise you also, reckon yourselves to be dead indeed to sin, but alive to God in Christ Jesus our Lord. Therefore do not let sin reign in your mortal body, that you should obey it in its lusts. And do not present your members as instruments of unrighteousness to sin, but present yourselves to God as being alive from the dead, and your members as instruments of righteousness to God. For sin shall not have dominion over you, for you are not under law but under grace.

We are freed from sin so that we **can** live a different life. We no longer have to live under sin's dominion because 1) Jesus paid the price for it, and 2) we, having died with Christ, are freed from the obligation of the slave-master relationship. When we were slaves to sin, we had no other option but to obey its commands. Romans 6:18 clarifies and expounds the matter for us, *"And having been set free from sin, you became slaves of righteousness."* If we no longer have to obey sin and are now "slaves to righteousness," we are **capable** of obeying God and **capable** of denying sin because God is now our master and lives in us.

The Way of the Cross

Jesus Christ invites us to live out the effective power of baptism every day. Just as baptism is a call to die to our sins, it is also a call to a lifestyle of death to ourselves and the carnality and sinful desires that creep in so subtly. Jesus calls us to live in the same manner He lived, which is to follow the pathway of the cross: *"Then Jesus said to His disciples, "If anyone desires to come after Me, let him deny himself, and take up his cross, and follow Me"* (Matthew 16:24).

Living in the way of the cross (dying to sin and denial of self), following as a disciple of Christ, sharing with Him in His death, and offering up ourselves to the Lord daily as a living sacrifice is extremely difficult. If living in such a way were easy, everyone would do it! It is true that Jesus took the punishment for our sins and He conquered them, but the reality is, we still live in our carnal self, and until we reach Heaven, our flesh will seek to return to its natural desire for sin. For this reason, Jesus invites us to consider ourselves *"dead to sin,"* (Romans 6:11).

We must consider ourselves dead to sin because if we live into sin again, it will inevitably produce death. Either we die to sin, or we let sin rise again and bring death to us— either way there will be death. One form brings life, and the other brings destruction. All sin is death, but death comes in different forms. Obviously there is physical death, but sin can cause the death of a family or a relationship. It can also cause the death of a clean conscience, the death of dreams, or the death of personal potential. Poor, carnal decisions and sin will invariably result in the death of something in our lives. However, in our participation in the death of Jesus, we unite to Him so death no longer has dominion over us, and we live in Jesus' abundant life (see Romans 6:14 and 23).

The Franks were a tribe of people that history knows as some of the "barbarians" that helped usher in the fall of the Roman Empire. In the year AD 496, the king of the Franks, Clovis, converted to Christianity. It was customary in the culture of the time that when the king converted, so did everyone else, many times under obligation. Such conversions are not of faith or conviction, but of expediency. Obligatory or expedient conversions—either then or today—produce nominal Christians that come nothing close to becoming actual disciples.

King Clovis obligated all of his subjects and warriors to be baptized into Christianity. However, when his warriors went under the water, they held their right hands up and out of the water. They refused to baptize this part of their body so that they could, in "good conscience" continue fighting and killing. The Franks exemplify a people who were baptized for expediency (though doubtless some in true faith) but were not committed to following the way of the Cross. We cannot live as we wish and still walk in the fullness of God's power and blessings. We cannot have our cake and eat it too!

I had the privilege of baptizing a friend who happens to be named Frank, and his story is the exact opposite of the warrior Franks! For several months since arriving at the church, God had been completely transforming his life. He had been walking out of a life of disbelief and sin. He confessed to me that, though having "believed" in the Lord, like the Franks of old, he was indifferent to sin and life change. As he sinned, he was content to simply offer a halfway sincere apology to God—and then keep on sinning. As he drew closer to God and attended church regularly, he found that the Holy Spirit was not letting him sin comfortably anymore. It was at that time he came to me and asked me to baptize him. This was his moment to give everything to Jesus and hold nothing back; to advance into a life of full victory and freedom from the devastating effects of sin; to bury in the water his past life of sin; to surrender fully to a new Master; and to offer his life as a sacrifice to the Lord and walk the way of the Cross.

The life as a living sacrifice to the Lord—living in the power of baptism—means that we give ourselves completely over to the Lord in every area of our lives and repenting of all our sins. Living a life of repentance as a living sacrifice to the Lord goes completely against our sinful, corrupt way of being. The old, wicked self looks to come back, and temptations and sinful desires are a reality to contend with. We squirrel away little, tiny sins in order to hide them from the Lord so that we can go back and enjoy them later. But living in the power of baptism means **not** going back to the things which Jesus' death has freed us from. We are free, and we have both the right and the power to live differently than how our former master of sin obligated us to. God has closed the sea over Pharaoh and drowned our sins and slavery in the waters, but we, also, must choose not to go back to slavery. That part of our life is dead to sin and, we are compelled to never go back to it.

IV

Baptism

The Waters of Resurrection

If salvation was nothing more than being forgiven of our sins and being spared an eternity of separation from God, that would be enough! In this we can see the greatness of God's generosity toward people, yet our salvation is much more than "getting to heaven" one day, or having "fire insurance." The purpose of God's salvation is to bring all of us back to the purposes for which we were created and to share in God's life and work with Him. When we rise with Jesus symbolically in baptism, the reality is that Jesus has not just forgiven us, but He is also bringing us into the fullness of life that He always desired for us! What a wonderful work of salvation!

A New Creation

When we are forgiven of our sins and begin a new life in Jesus, the Bible says that we are *"born again."* Think about that metaphor for just a moment. The moment we are born we are helpless infants. The fact that we are simply born and alive is a wonderful thing, but that is not the culmination of life! Our parents did not leave us at the hospital when we were born saying, "Well, our work is done!" The birth is only the beginning.

At birth we don't know how to do anything. We cannot speak, feed ourselves, walk, or have the knowledge for **anything** that life requires for successful living. We don't even know there is a whole world out there in which we have to learn to live.

It is the same with us spiritually as we begin an new life in Jesus. It is a wonderful thing to be born again, but being born into the Kingdom of God requires a new way of living, walking, talking, and feeding. Everything about this new life has to be learned, which requires growth. We have died to our sins in baptism, but we are also resurrected into this new life. Our spiritual birth is only the beginning.

Romans 6:4 declares, *"Therefore we were buried with Him through baptism into death, that just as Christ was raised from the dead by the glory of the Father, even so we also should walk in newness of life."* Just as the death of Jesus is powerful and effective for the forgiveness of sins, the resurrection of Jesus is powerful and effective for living a brand new life. In baptism, we have both died and been resurrected to new life with Jesus Christ. Being immersed in the water and rising up again from it symbolizes this death and resurrection with Jesus Christ. We have already seen how baptism is symbolic for our salvation, but the symbolism is more than being saved from our sins, it is also rising to the new life for which we have been saved and which God is making effective in us through Jesus.

In John 20, we find the narrative of Jesus' resurrection beginning with these words: *"Now on the first day of the week..."* On the surface, these words would seem little more than an indication of the timing of the story so that the author can advance the central point of the narrative by giving greater context to the reader. However, these few words give a profound understanding of Jesus' resurrection. The Apostle John is reminding us of another "first day of the week." The last time God did something new on the "first day of the week" was during the creation of the world in Genesis 1.

In the biblical creation story, seven times God calls His own creation "good." In His goodness, God created humankind to participate in the oversight of this earth. Yet because of the disobedience of Adam and his wife, to whom were given the stewardship of the earth, the world that God first created was messed up, for Adam and his wife were the ones who permitted the entrance of sin and death into God's good creation. As a result, all of creation—humanity included—is contaminated by sin and death while God had created us to participate in the fullness of His goodness, purity and life.

When Jesus Christ died on the cross and was laid in a tomb, He took with Him all the disorder of the messed-up-world along with the death penalty that you and I deserve for our sins. When He rose from the dead, both sin and death stayed in that tomb. Only one figure came out victorious—Jesus Christ! When Jesus came out of the tomb on the "first day of the week," the Apostle John is indicating to us that this is the first day of a new creation. Colossians 1:18 says, "*And He is...the beginning, the firstborn from the dead, that in all things He may have the preeminence.*" Jesus is the ***first*** to rise from the dead. If He is the first, then there must be more to follow—that would be you and me!

With Jesus we live again, passing from the life of the old creation to the redeemed life in the new creation that God has brought about in Jesus Christ. 2 Corinthians 5:17 tells us, "*Therefore, if anyone is in Christ, he is a new creation; old things have passed away; behold, all things have become new.*" In our union with Jesus in His death and resurrection, we are rising to begin a new life, in a new Kingdom, and with a new King over us.

Salvation and new life in Christ Jesus occurs in a single moment and continues expanding in a never-ending line through eternity. God forgives our sins and initiates a new life the instant we repent of our sins and put our faith in Jesus Christ. But from there, God continues to develop and unveil the purpose for our salvation during the rest of our lives. God's work in us is an ever-continuing process of growth and development. Upon entering this new creation and this new Kingdom, we must learn how to live again. The former ways of thinking and being in the life of the "old creation" have no place in the "new creation." Resurrection life is completely different than the old life.

In keeping with the understanding of baptism as both death and resurrection, Ephesians 5:14 quotes what is most likely an early Christian hymn saying, *"Awake, you who sleep, arise from the dead, and Christ will give you light."* Scholars believe this maxim may have been used during baptisms. The context of Ephesians 5:14 is that of coming out of the darkness and living in the light of Christ Jesus. The darkness of the death of sin, which enshrouded us, is now blown apart by the resurrection power of Jesus Christ, which awakens us to the light of God's living presence.

This resurrection power living in and through us permits us to walk differently in this dark, sin-infested world. We can walk differently because we can now see! Jesus has given us light. We are no longer infested by the darkness of the world around us. Since we are risen with Christ Jesus, His life and light dwell in us making us the light of the world. The resurrection of Jesus in us, symbolized in our baptism, allows us to *"walk circumspectly, not as fools but as wise, redeeming the time, because the days are evil"* (Ephesians 5:15-16). In Jesus Christ, we are now able to live as new creations.

New Creation, New Light

I want us to go deeper into the meaning of "Christ will give you light." This phrase is particularly significant in the understanding of being baptized and entering into the full, living reality of salvation and new life. In baptism we are a new creation. Jesus died and was resurrected as the first born from the dead and the focal point of the new creation. We find even more significance for our new life in Jesus through the creation story. In baptism, we follow Him in this death, resurrection, and new creation. As a new creation who is now living in the light of Jesus, let us go back and see the connection of Creator God's original creation to the new creation.

The first four words God speaks in the Bible are, *"Let there be light,"* (Genesis 1:3). In the utter chaos of the dark and yet-to-be-created world, God calls light into existence as the first order of business. It is interesting that light is introduced before the creation of the planets or stars. Light is much deeper than what the dictionary says as, "electromagnetic radiation to which the organs of sight react." Light is who God is, and His light is more than something that gives us the ability to see physical objects around us. Light is also spiritual.

In those first four loaded words, it is as if God is declaring who He is and what He desires through the creation of light: Let there be the understanding of Me; let there be knowledge; let there be My presence; let there be wisdom; let there be clarity. Such things are the result of spiritual light. The very next verse begins by revealing God's character in this light: the light is good. One cannot create something that is not a part of their being. If the light is good, then the Creator of it is also good.

The very next action God takes is to separate the light from the darkness, (Genesis 1:4). This separation of the two is not merely to give us day and night. In dividing between them, God also gives understanding to whom He is and whom He is not. There is such a thing as light—the good light of the Creator, but there is also such a thing as darkness—and God unequivocally distinguishes between the two. There is good, and there is evil. There is right, and there is wrong. There is illumination, and there is confusion. There is a created order, and there is a perverted order.

The Light of the World

In the book of John, the Apostle refers to Jesus as the Word and the Light throughout the Gospel. The two are inseparable, as he writes in John 1:1-5 and 14:

In the beginning was the Word, and the Word was with God, and the Word was God. He was in the beginning with God. All things were made through Him, and without Him nothing was made that was made. In Him was life, and the life was the light of men. And the light shines in the darkness, and the darkness did

*not comprehend it...and the Word became flesh
and dwelt among us, and we beheld His
glory...*

Just as God's spoken Word brought the Light into
existence in the beginning and brought order to the
dark chaos, the opening words to the Gospel of John
remind us of the very beginning of creation. In the
chaos of a world dark with sin, the same Word and
Light became incarnate in Jesus. God's Word and
Light, in Jesus Christ, are creating a new beginning for
humanity.

It is this same Person who cries out "I am the Light of
the world!" (John 8:12). God's Word brings life and
light to mankind. In the utter chaos and darkness of a
world steeped in sin, God sends the Light of the World,
His own Son, Jesus Christ, to help us see life as God
intended it to be. The good light of the good Creator
illuminates things, not as we wish them to be, but as
Creator designed them to be. In the light of Jesus' life,
we understand how God designed our lives to function.
The theologian C.S. Lewis brilliantly observed, "I
believe in Christianity as I believe that the sun has
risen: not only because I see it, but because by it I see
everything else."

The Defining Light

Nothing in our universe contains any color in and of
itself. The color of the shirt you are wearing at this

moment is not contained in the essence of the material. If your shirt appears to be blue—it is not actually blue— it is nothing. The science of color tells us that every color of the spectrum is contained in white light. The color that we perceive with our eyes is actually the color in the light spectrum that bounces off an object. Color is light. Hence, where there is no light, all is darkness. If anything had color in and of itself, then darkness would not affect it.

An easy experiment illustrating this fact is to take something green or blue, go into a dark room and shine a red light on it. The object will look black or grayish depending on the hue. Since red light does not have green or blue in its spectrum, no green or blue light is present to bounce off the object.

In a dark world, the Light of Jesus not only shines—*it defines*. In Revelation 19:12, the resurrected Jesus is described with "eyes like flames of fire." **Light does not define Jesus, Jesus is the source of the light who give definition.** When we decide to let our world be defined by anything that is not the light of Jesus, we are incapable of seeing any issue as God understands it. Our vision is muddied, unclear, and confused.

As with the experiment with the red light, it is interesting to note how two people can look at the same object, but the light by which the object is illuminated determines their perception of the object. A person who, for instance, looks at the issue of abortion through the light of the world will come to very different conclusions than the person who looks at it through the light of Jesus. Consider what the prophet Isaiah warns us about devastating consequences walking in a different light, or in the light of our own personal preferences rather than in the clarity God provides:

Who among you fears the Lord? Who obeys the voice of His Servant? Who walks in darkness and has no light? Let him trust in the name of the Lord and rely upon his God. Look, all you who...walk in the light of your fire...This you shall have from My hand: you shall lie down in torment. (Isaiah 50:10-11)

Every person has a choice to make: By which light will I choose to walk? There is always another light. There is always a way to try and manipulate the light of God so that one sees what one desires to see. If we do not like all the colors of God's spectrum, we can take the certain colors we like and, like the red light, define everything by it with utter disregard for the **totality** of God's revelation. For this reason, there are sectors of the Church that interpret some of God's laws according to current thought when the Bible is clear on the subject. Some desire to twist the light to make it reflect what is most convenient to them.

In the book of Ezekiel, we find one of the most terrifying, non-sugarcoated passages of Scripture regarding the light by which one chooses to walk:

Now some of the elders of Israel came to me and sat before me. And the word of the Lord came to me, saying, "Son of man, these men have set up their idols in their hearts, and put before them that which causes them to stumble into iniquity. Should I let Myself be inquired of at all by them? "Therefore speak to them, and say to them, 'Thus says the Lord God: "Everyone of the house of Israel who sets up his idols in his heart, and puts before him what causes him to stumble into iniquity, and then comes to the prophet, I the Lord will answer him who comes, according to the multitude of his idols..." (Ezekiel 14:1-4)

People set up idols for themselves. They shine the light of their desires, bias, preconceived ideas, and selfish ambitions upon everything they do. People do this so well that they will actually persuade themselves that the light of their own will is indeed the light of God's will. Where there is stubbornness, lack of repentance, and self-will, God will allow a person to continue in their darkness while they continue believing they walk in God's light.

A prime example of choosing to walk in one's own light comes from the much-venerated father of psychiatry, Sigmund Freud, who understood well the problem of human depression, yet whose ultimate solution turned out to be a different kind of light. Freud writes that one of the sources of human depression is that humanity is incapable of attaining the moral standards set for us. This produces a feeling of inadequacy, guilt, shame, and thus, depression. It is worth noting that the moral standards at the time of Freud's writing were quite different than they are today. Part of this decline of standards has to do with Freud's next proposition.

Sadly, Freud was on the cusp of stumbling onto the brilliant solution God had given humanity when he went the opposite way. Freud was right in his analysis that humanity cannot attain God's righteous, moral standards. This is why God sent Jesus Christ to fulfill them and die for our sins so that in Him we can live as God wants. That is the message of the Gospel! God has done for us what none of us could do on our own.

Freud's solution was not in Christ, but rather to change the standards! In other words, if we cannot live up to the standard, then let us redefine the standard to our liking. Who defines the standards, anyway? When I get to define the standards—then I can never be wrong! Problem solved. Actually, there is a much greater problem created—it is a redefinition of the light. God is the ultimate standard—He is the definition of the light by which we live.

Fully Opening to the Light

One summer, my wife and I went on a vacation in her hometown of Puerto Vallarta, Mexico. As I was enjoying a little bit of sunbathing on the beach, my wife, who had gone on a walk down the beach, came back jubilant with three new pairs of earrings she bought from a vendor on the beach. Our budget was fairly tight, so I asked her how much she had spent. She was very proud of her haggling skills and of the deal she just got. She triumphantly announced, "The man wanted to sell them to me for $7 each. I said that was too much so he made me a deal: Three sets for $21!" I rolled my eyes and did the math with her. "That cheater!" she shouted. We have laughed for years about that!

No one likes a cheater. No one likes a dishonest vendor. Probably all of us, at one point or another, have had an experience with dishonesty in buying something. This is the essence of what Jesus said in Mathew 6:22-23:

The lamp of the body is the eye. If therefore your eye is good, your whole body will be full of light. But if your eye is bad, your whole body will be full of darkness. If therefore the light that is in you is darkness, how great is that darkness!

The phrase, "if...your eye is good" does not indicate one's ability to see well, but has to do with one's capacity to be open and honest. The Greek word for "good" is "haplous." Haplous means singular and sincere[4], unfolded and undivided. It carries the idea of a person being open, honest, and without any other ulterior motive. It is a person who is sincere and wholehearted in all he or she does. Ephesians 6:5-6 talks about being obedient with *"sincerity of heart...not with eyeservice, as men-pleasers, but...doing the will of God from the heart."*

The insinuation of this word in the context of Ephesians 6 and Matthew 6 is that there is utter sincerity, openness, honesty, integrity, and simplicity of devotion to the Lord and solidarity in our personal character in all we do and in everything we are. We are to be people who say what we mean and mean what we say. We are to be singular of mind, unified in the intent of our heart, and totally integrated in our physical life and spiritual walk with Christ.

In contrast to the word haplous, imagine a man who is selling a piece of material or a garment which he knows has some sort of blemish on it. As he shows it off in order to sell it, he skillfully manipulates the material to purposely cover up the stain. Once he has convinced his customer and makes the sale, he throws up the "All Sales Final" sign before the buyer realizes what has happened.[5]

There are areas in each of our lives that we do not want exposed to the light. There are areas of embarrassment, shame, or habits that we desperately try to hold on to while convincing ourselves that the darkness of our secret sins are compatible with the light of Jesus Christ. When we hide pockets of darkness in our hearts, we are not open, wholehearted, nor singular in our being. Like the swindling merchant, we skillfully manipulate our hearts and lives so that people see only the good, godly, and virtuous side of us. Yet once we are alone, all the secret sins make their way to the surface, and we convince ourselves that we are walking fully in the light, when in reality, we are walking only in the light that is most comfortable for us.

Haplous—the "good" eye—is the honest unfolding of every area of one's soul before God. Nothing is hidden or skillfully manipulated. We are wholeheartedly giving everything that we are to Jesus, and everything about us is exposed to the light. Just as there is no darkness in God, there is to be no darkness in us, either.

The light of Jesus in us gives revelation, definition, and healing. The light of Jesus reveals the state of our sinfulness, and the darkness that is hidden inside. The light then defines what the sin is and what God requires of us. With revelation and definition comes healing. God does not want to humiliate us, but He does call us to repent of our sins. This is His call to the waters of baptism. As we enter in, we are immersed in Him—completely soaked in water; all sinfulness washed away and rising to walk in His light.

Resurrection Toward God's Promises

As the new life through the resurrection has continued meaning in the creation story, so it has continued instruction through the story of Israel. We have seen a type of baptism of the Israelites when they walked through the Red Sea, and this point of baptism was to forever close behind them their past life of slavery to sin. However, there was another type of baptism they went through as they entered into the Promised Land. This is not a different baptism, but rather a fuller picture of all the power and promise that is released to us as we go into the waters.

Under the leadership of Joshua, the entire nation of Israel was going to enter into a new land of promise and fruitfulness—in the same way we pass into the new life of a new creation. However, the flooded Jordan River stood between them and God's promise. Just as God opened up the waters of the Red Sea, He opened up the waters of the Jordan River in order that His people could walk through. This time it was not for freedom from slavery but to entrance into the full promise of God for a new life. The Israelite deliverance from slavery in Egypt was not simply to set them free and let them go their own way. They were brought **_out_** of Egypt in order to be brought **_in_** to God's full promises, life, blessing, and partnership.

The account of God bringing the Israelites in to His promise through Joshua's leadership is no coincidence with the narrative of Jesus' baptism. Let us briefly take into account a few parallels between the two stories.

The point of the Israelite's crossing of the Jordan River into the Promised Land had to be somewhere near the place where the Jordan empties into the Dead Sea. We know this because the Israelites first camp in the Promised Land was at Gilgal, and Gilgal is located a little more than a mile east of Jericho.[6] Furthermore, Jericho was the first battle the Israelites had in the land. Thus, the crossing must have been just above the Dead Sea.

Today, the popular site for pilgrims to be baptized in Jesus' footsteps in the Holy Land is located about 65 miles to the north of the Dead Sea where the Sea of Galilee forms the Jordan River. Let me assure you, Jesus was not baptized there. We can know this for two primary reasons. 1) John the Baptist was part of a religious community located down by the Dead Sea. He was also a preacher in the desert, which the Judean Desert is by the Dead Sea and Jericho. 2) People from Jerusalem came down to hear John the Baptist preach and to be baptized by him.. Jerusalem is only about 15 miles from Jericho, 20 miles from the Jordan River. In short, ***Jesus was baptized by John the Baptist at the same place Israel, led by Joshua, crossed into the Promised Land.*** What is more, the Hebrew names Joshua (Y-sh-a) and Jesus (Y-sh-a) are, in fact, the same name, both meaning "salvation"!

What an amazing picture of baptism! As Joshua (Yoshua) lead Israel into a new land through the waters of the Jordan River, at the same place, nearly 1500 years later, Jesus (Yeshua) is coming through the waters to lead God's people into a new Kingdom![7] Jesus is coming to fulfill for the whole world what God began among the Israelites.

The symbols of resurrection and entrance into the promises of God that baptism represents, paint for us a larger picture of what our identification with Jesus' death and resurrection produce. In His death, we are freed from sin, and in His resurrection, we are brought into new life with God and into the fullness of His abundant promises.

We find the narrative of Jesus Christ's baptism in Matthew 3:13-17:

*Then Jesus came from Galilee to John at the Jordan to be baptized by him. And John tried to prevent Him, saying, 'I need to be baptized by You, and are You coming to me?' But Jesus answered and said to him, 'Permit it to be so now, for thus it is fitting for us **to fulfill all righteousness**.' Then he allowed Him. When He had been baptized, Jesus came up immediately from the water; and behold, the heavens were opened to Him, and He saw the Spirit of God descending like a dove and alighting upon Him. And suddenly a voice came from heaven, saying, "This is My beloved Son, in whom I am well pleased."*

When Jesus was baptized, four events occurred that we will study in more detail. 1) Jesus fulfilled righteousness; 2) The heavens opened up to Him; 3) The Holy Spirit descended upon Him; and 4) A voice from heaven declared God's pleasure with His obedience affirming Him as God's Son. In the following chapters we are going to look at these four events as they go hand-in-hand with the new resurrection life that we have in Christ. We will begin with the first event in this chapter.

To Fulfill All Righteousness

In the Greek language, which is the original language in which the New Testament was written, the word for "baptize" that is used is "baptidzo," and this is an intensified version of the root word "bapto."[8] Bapto is to dip something, such as a chip in salsa or an article of clothing in water. "Baptidzo" is also used for a ship sinking in the ocean or for the sailors who go down to a watery grave in a shipwreck. It means to "go under" and to "perish."[9] In this way, we can also understand baptism as our former life completely perishing under the waters.

However, Jesus was baptized without having sinned, unlike you and me. Jesus had nothing to repent from, rather He was baptized in obedience to God and "to fulfill all righteousness." The righteousness that was fulfilled in His baptism was the total submission of Himself to the will of God. Jesus is completely God, but He was also completely human. Jesus was like us, but without sin (Hebrews 4:15). He had His own will, thoughts, desires, and emotions. When He entered the waters of baptism, He was making the conscious decision to deny Himself and follow the will of God. In effect, He allowed His own fleshly humanity to drown in the water so that He would live completely to God.

We can clearly see the results of Jesus' full submission to God's perfect will several times in the gospels. Five times in the book of John, Jesus makes the statement that His words and actions are only what He hears the Father saying and sees the Father doing. In John 5:19 Jesus says,

I say to you, the Son can do nothing of Himself, unless it is something He sees the Father doing." "I can do nothing of my own initiative" (5:30); *"I can do nothing on my own initiative, but I speak these things as the Father taught Me"* (8:28); *"For I did not speak on My own initiative"* (12:49); *"I do not speak on My own initiative, but the Father abiding in Me does His works* (14:10).

Most notable in Jesus' perfect life of submission is His struggle in the Garden of Gethsemane. Only minutes before His betrayal and hours before His crucifixion, He asks the Father if there is another way to accomplish His will, seeking that "this cup may pass" from Him. He goes on to say, *"nevertheless not My will but Yours be done"* (Luke 22:42).

This is the life that God desires for us—a life that experiences the delivering power from sin and death and the living power of the resurrection. It is only in our total submission to God that we can live in His power. It is one of the great paradoxes of new life in Jesus—in order to gain life, we first lose it, and in order to have authority, we first submit all of ourselves to God. The implication is that we die with the purpose of living again—but living **His** life! The great theologian C.S. Lewis explains this purposeful living in his book *Mere Christianity*:

The Christian way is different: harder, and easier. Christ says: Give me All. I don't want so much of your time and so much of your money and so much of your work: I want You. I have not come to torment your natural self, but to kill it. No half-measures are any good. I don't want to cut off a branch here and a branch there, I want to have the whole tree down. I don't want to drill the tooth, or crown it, or stop it, but to have it out. Hand over the whole natural self, all the desires which you think innocent as well as the ones you think wicked— the whole outfit. I will give you a new self instead. In fact, I will give you Myself: my own will shall become yours.[10]

The resurrection is a **promise** for the future and eternal life with God, but it is also the **power** of God made available for us right now—a promise for tomorrow and power for today! In 1 Peter 1:3-4, the Apostle Peter makes the following declaration:

Blessed be the God and Father of our Lord
Jesus Christ, who according to His abundant
mercy has begotten us again to a living hope
through the resurrection of Jesus Christ from
the dead, to an inheritance incorruptible and
undefiled and that does not fade away,
reserved in heaven for you.

Along with the promise of **life then**, Peter continues
telling us of the power of God available for **life now**:

As His divine power has given to us all things
that pertain to life and godliness, through the
knowledge of Him who called us by glory and
virtue, by which have been given to us
exceedingly great and precious promises, that
through these you may be partakers of the
divine nature, having escaped the corruption
that is in the world through lust. (2 Peter 1:3-4)

The working of God in our lives does not end with
baptism—quite the contrary! His power is released in
us! The life and power of God are available to us right
now through the resurrection of Jesus. When we unite
ourselves to His resurrection in baptism, sin and death
hold no sway over us, (Romans 6:12-14).

We have the privilege to participate **right now** in all
the power, the resources, and the life that God has
promised us in Heaven. But before we go to Heaven to

be with Him, we can experience Heaven becoming a reality in our world right now—Heaven on earth! In fact, Jesus Himself told us to pray this way, *"Your Kingdom come, your will be done **on earth as it is in Heaven**."* (Matthew 6:10). 2 Corinthians 1:22 affirms that God *"has sealed us and given us the Spirit in our hearts as a guarantee"* of all the life and promises to come that He has in store for us. The purpose of our identification with the life of Jesus is so that we would live the power of God and the promises of tomorrow in our daily lives!

V

Baptism

Preparation, Purification, and Participation

As we enter the waters of baptism, God does a profound work in us. In our salvation He works more than the forgiveness of sins, He generously invites us to live in all the benefits of this salvation. In John 10:10, Jesus states that He has come to give us *"life and life abundantly."* In Jesus Christ, God is inviting us into more than a state of reconciliation; He invites us to live out the complete purpose for which we are saved. He invites us to ***prepare*** ourselves to see Him; He invites us into a life of ***purity*** from the effects sin has left on our lives; and He invites us to ***participate*** in the abundant life He always intended us to live.

Philippians 3:12 gives a profound understanding of the depth of our salvation in saying, *"Not that I have already attained, or am already perfected; but I press on, that I may lay hold of that for which Christ Jesus has also laid hold of me."* In other words, there is the recognition of imperfection of our current human status, the ongoing work of God healing the brokenness that sin left behind in us, as well as the acknowledgement that there is a larger purpose for which God has saved us that needs to be actively pursued and laid hold of.

Preparation

The second event in the baptism of Jesus, after "fulfilling all righteousness," was that the heavens were opened to Him (Matthew 3:16). We do not know exactly what happened at that moment, but we probably all have in our minds a grandiose picture of all the clouds in the sky parting off to either side of the heavens, a singular ray of sun shining down upon Jesus, and a chorus of heavenly music filling all who witnessed this baptism. Neither you nor I were there and maybe it did happen that way—but I doubt it!

We have already discussed the fact that baptism is a symbol of a new creation, yet there is a striking connection between the fall of humanity into sin and the recovery of humanities purposes in God's life through baptism, and it has to do with the heavens being opened.

The first creation was spoiled by the sin of a man and woman, who in their rebellion against God's instruction, took for themselves that which did not belong to them. Such disregard for God's Word and arrogance to suppose their limited understanding would trump that of the Almighty God, did, in a sense, accomplish what they were looking for. They desired— coveted—knowledge beyond their own. Upon eating the forbidden fruit, *"**Then the eyes of both of them were opened**, and they realized they were naked. And they sewed fig leaves together and made themselves loincloths."* (Genesis 3:7).

Rebellion against God suddenly opened their eyes to the shame and consequences of sin. Disobedience gives revelation to a way of living that ultimately brings destruction. You have seen this before, either in your own life, or the life of someone you know: How moments of indulgence in selfish sin that go either uncaught or undisciplined, give license to further destructive habits in a person's life. Like seemingly innocuous "gateway drugs," they give revelation or desire for the harder stuff that devastates the human body and soul. Little sins tend to beget bigger sins. In the case of the first couple in the Garden, a moment of rebellion opened their eyes to their folly and the terrible cost of sin, which enslaved all humanity.

In contrast to the fall of the first creation, Jesus came to inaugurate a brand new creation in which He offers us a chance to take part. As Jesus came out of the water "fulfilling all righteousness," He was doing the opposite of Adam and Eve. He was not rebelling against God, He was fully submitting to Him. As the first couple's eyes were opened to sin **through disobedience**, Jesus' eyes were opened to the heavenly realm **through obedience**. As Adam and Eve were degraded from a dimension of authority to slavery **through rebellion**, Jesus entered into a new dimension of spiritual awareness and insight **through submission**. The submission of Jesus to God in baptism opened new dimensions of life for Him. When the Bible says that the heavens were opened to Jesus, He had a new clarity of the spiritual realm—a new ability to see a greater revelation of God. His baptism was preparation for a new life of intimacy with the Father, whereas Adam's life was cut off from God.

Perhaps you are thinking that this is impossible because Jesus was the Son of God and there was no way that Jesus would have needed any such enhancement. It is true that Jesus is the Son of God. However, we have to remember that Jesus became a man—a human just like you and me. In my years as a pastor and Bible College professor, I have found that many believers have a difficult time understanding the fact that Jesus was indeed fully human and lived as we do. It is much easier to understand Jesus as the divine Son of God made flesh without taking time to appreciate the fact that _Jesus actually had flesh_. Luke 2:52 gives us a clue as to Jesus' humanity and His growth in understanding who He was and what God was doing through Him: *"And Jesus increased in wisdom and stature, and in favor with God and men."* In other words, the Son of God was also the Son of Man living as we do. When Jesus spoke His first words, they were not, "Mother, I am the Son of God!" Jesus Himself grew mentally, physically, spiritually, and socially. In His growing up years, He would have come to the realization of whom He was.

Paul declares the following about Jesus in Philippians 2:6-7, *"who being in the form of God, did not consider it robbery to be equal with God, but made Himself of no reputation, taking the form of a bondservant, and coming in the likeness of men."* In other words, He lived just as we do. He did not draw off of His divinity in order to conquer life in the flesh—He conquered life in the flesh through His submission and obedience to God. Jesus, as fully man, needed God's help just like we do. Jesus, too, needed to "see God" in a new revelation and power in order to fulfill His work here on earth.

In Matthew 5:8, Jesus teaches, *"Blessed are the pure in heart, for they will see God."* What is more, Psalm 24:3-4 asserts, *"Who may ascend into the hill of the Lord? Or who may stand in His holy place? He who has clean hands and a pure heart..."* A link exists between the purity of our hearts before Him and the ability to see God at a new dimension, to understand Him, to deepen our lives in Him, and to have more revelation of His being. In other words, our commitment to walk in righteousness before Him and *"abstain from fleshly lusts which war against the soul"* (1 Peter 2:11), allows for a deeper fellowship and intimacy with God.

Psalm 25:14 instructs us, *"The friendship of the Lord is for those who fear him, and he makes his covenant known to them"* (NRSV). The intimate revelations of God and a deeper friendship with Him is a privilege reserved for those who fear Him, honor Him, and who have "clean hands and a pure heart." In one sense, when we come to Christ Jesus for salvation, all of us are His friends. However, neither you nor I would share the most intimate details of our lives with just any friend but only with those worthy of such confidence. God reserves such intimate friendship for those He can trust. This is what happened in Jesus' baptism. In His humanity, He had a deeper communion with the Father, due to having submitted Himself in baptism. It may sound odd that Jesus the Son of God needed a deeper revelation in the spiritual realm, but we must remember that He was completely human and experienced life the same as we do. In baptism, God does the same for us. A simple step of obedience to Father God demonstrates our desire for deeper friendship with Him.

God, too, wants to have a deeper and more open relationship with each of us. Baptism is preparation to see Him. If we have already been baptized, we must be diligent to cultivate a dynamic and growing relationship with Him because He has more to reveal to us! It is not that we work for His love, rather we are becoming more intimate friends with Him as we continually live a life that pleases Him. The more like

Him we are, the more He entrusts us with an intimate revelation of Himself. In this way, we will begin to "see God" move in our personal lives as well in our churches. "Blessed are the pure in heart;" they will see God move and reveal Himself like never before!

Purification

In preparation to see God in a new way with a pure heart, it is God who needs to purify us so that we **can** see Him. Through our salvation, Jesus cleansed us so we stand forgiven of our sins through the cross and His blood. But even beyond forgiveness, God wants to wash us from the ugliness of sin that has marked our lives. You can be forgiven but still live with the residual effects of sin. When Jesus said that He needed to "fulfill all righteousness," He was taking things that were unrighteous, the "un right," and making them "right" in our lives. Where the brokenness of sin has warped and damaged our ways of thinking and acting, and where they do not mesh with God's revealed way of living, God is working to purify and renew us in His pure righteousness.

As in the first Passover when the Israelites put the blood of the lamb over the door, Jesus put His blood over us and saved us from slavery and death. Now that we are saved, His blood needs to be applied to the inside of the house. He needs to come in and wash all that is dirty **inside** the house!

Every house has piles of dirty clothes that need to be washed—we are six in my house and it seems like the hamper overflows everyday! Likewise we all have the dirty clothes of behaviors, habits, and faulty mentalities in our lives that should not be there. These are the effects of sin that we hold on to such as pornography, alcohol and other addictions, excessive eating, lying, manipulating, selfish ambitions, unforgiveness, hatred, and other such things with which we may struggle. Jesus didn't just come to save us from our sin and brokenness, He also came to wash us clean from them.

There are four words in the Greek language that refer to the washing of the body for the sake of purity: *nipto, louo, katharos, and baptidzo.* These words became synonymous with ritual purification of the body in preparation for religious purposes.[11] 1 John 1:9 says, *"If we confess our sins, He is faithful and just to forgive us our sins and purify [katharidzo; katharos] us from all unrighteousness."*

In the Hebrew, the word for washing, *kabas,* means simply "to wash" as we understand it, but it is different than bathing the body. It denotes the washing of clothing under the water; to do the job of a purifier.[12] The removal of our sin is in the cross, but in baptism there is a purification, scrubbing clean, and renewal from the lingering effects that sin has marked on our lives. These are the persistent consequences of the former ways of thinking and the habits that have carried over from the past life that seek to drag us away from the new life we have in Christ.

The Lord tells us in Isaiah 1:18, *"Come now, and let us reason together, says the Lord, though your sins are like scarlet, they shall be as white as snow…"* Likewise in his Psalm of repentance, King David asks God to **forgive** him, but he also asks God to **wash** him. *"Wash [kabas] me thoroughly from my iniquity and cleanse me from my sin"* (Psalm 51:2). The blood of Jesus Christ is enough for our forgiveness of sins, redemption from slavery, and entrance into God's family—as Israel was freed from Egypt. Although Israel was out of Egypt, God still had much work to do to remove Egypt from them! When we come to Christ and are freed from the power of sin, God then goes to work to get all traces us sin out of us.

In order to establish His covenant with His people, God took Israel to Mt. Sinai. This moment was indelibly marked in the calling and mentality of Israel. It was the moment when God descended upon the mountain, revealed Himself, established His covenant, and gave Israel His laws by which to live—the Ten Commandments. But before the revelation, look at what God instructed them to do in Exodus 19:10-11, *"Go to the people and consecrate them today and tomorrow, and let them wash [kabas] their clothes. And let them be ready for the third day. For on the third day the Lord will come down upon Mount Sinai in the sight of all the people."* There was a time of **preparation** and **purification** before the *revelation*.

This reminds me of a defining moment in the life of my sister. Ever since we were kids, she had the habit of keeping her room untidy. Every Saturday, our mom gave us a list of chores to do, and without fail, the first chore was to clean our bedrooms. My sister would literally take *all day* to do a chore that should have taken twenty minutes. When she was about 15 or 16, something changed in her and it happened because of an encounter with God.

My sister loved God—and still does—with all her heart. One day she went into her dirty room to have a personal devotional time with God. As she opened her Bible, the Holy Spirit spoke very clearly to her: "You want me to meet with you...*here*?" That was all He said, but the message was unmistakable: God wants every area of our lives clean and in order because He is clean and orderly. *(As a matter of fact, that has been my wife's motto about our house ever since we have been married, "Everything clean and in order!").*

As soon as my sister heard those words, she immediately began to clean her room to make it an acceptable place for her to meet with the Lord. You can imagine the shock our mom had when she walked by her room and actually saw her cleaning it!

This is not to say that we need to get everything right and all cleaned up in our lives in order for God to come and be with us. We come to Jesus and He does that for us. These are not **rules** to follow in blind legalism as if we simply clean the house and all would be well in life. Following exterior rules does not produce an interior change. But the cleanliness of the presentation of ourselves to God is an exterior **result** of the interior cleansing that God has worked in us.

The ancient Jewish philosopher Philo, in talking about certain religious people, said *"They remove dirt from their bodies by baths and means of purification, but they neither desire nor seek to wash away the passions of their souls by which life is soiled."*[13] In this same way, Jesus reprimanded some Pharisees for excessive adherence to the ritual of hand washing when, on the spiritual side, they never took care to make sure their hearts were clean. He said to them, *"There is nothing that enters a man from outside which can defile him; but the things which come out of him, those are the things that defile a man"* (Mark 7:15).

We can no longer live in the things of our former life, nor allow their contamination when we have been forgiven. We must be both forgiven and cleansed. Jesus wants to wash us of such things so that we become completely His. Paul goes on to teach in Colossians 2:11-12 about the cleansing effects of baptism:

In Him you were also circumcised with the circumcision made without hands, by putting off the body of the sins of the flesh, by the circumcision of Christ, buried with Him in baptism, in which you also were raised with Him through faith in the working of God, who raised Him from the dead.

1 Peter 3:20-21 also says:

who formerly were disobedient, when once the Divine longsuffering waited in the days of Noah, while the ark was being prepared, in which a few, that is, eight souls, were saved through water. There is also an antitype which now saves us—baptism (not the removal of the filth of the flesh, but the answer of a good conscience toward God), through the resurrection of Jesus Christ.

There is no condemnation for those who are in Christ, but God does expect His people to live according to His ways. Baptism is the place where Jesus purifies us so that we are able to "see God."

The symbolic work of baptism is a life-long process of cleansing. Though cleansed from sin, there are moments where we continue to battle temptations and the brokenness of our past ways of thinking and being. Though made holy in Christ Jesus and instantaneously saved from our sins, God's ongoing work in us continually delivers us from past effects of sin.

Health, healing, deliverance, wholeness, purity, and freedom from sin are continual processes of the Spirit's work in us. They also require a continual working out on our part. The fact of physical life in the flesh in a sinful world is that we will still keep fighting the urges of the flesh. Yet, even in this we see the spiritual power of what happened in our salvation and baptism at work. We have died to sin so we can live for Christ. Galatians 5:16 encourages us in how to walk in a life of freedom: *"Walk in the Spirit, and you shall not fulfill the lust of the flesh."*

If you broke your leg and went to the doctor to get it set and put in a cast, you would not leave the doctor's office jumping and running. There is a process of healing that needs to happen before a full recovery is made. It is the same with believers. We come to the cross and are saved by the blood of Jesus, and we are symbolically washed in the waters of baptism. God takes our lives through the very long process of total healing. And there is something of this restored life that is not attained until we submit ourselves in obedience to the Lord in the waters of baptism. As said earlier in this book, "When we are immersed in the waters of baptism and welcome this new, supernatural way of living, it is in essence, the gateway into the process of learning to live as a disciple of Jesus Christ."

In the beginning, we were made in God's image and likeness, but our relationship with Him and His life flowing into us, like an umbilical cord from a mother to the baby in her womb, was broken due to sin, and we spiritually died. In the death and resurrection of Jesus Christ, our relationship with God is restored. Though forgiven, we still have areas of brokenness in us that the process of the Holy Spirit's work continues to restore. This life-long process of *"working out our salvation"* (Philippians 2:12) through the strength and care of the Holy Spirit continually working, correcting, and guiding us which puts back together the pieces of our life that were broken by sin.

A River of Humility

Lest we think that this work of purification is impossible and life completely free from sin in unreachable, let me assure you that it is...for us. It is God who must do this work in us and *for us.* All of us can relate to the story of Naaman, a Syrian general who suffered leprosy. When he heard that there was a prophet in Israel who healed people, he searched him out. Elisha, the prophet, sent him to bathe seven times in the Jordan River to be cleansed. The prideful general, however, had other ideas upon hearing the order:

But Naaman became furious, and went away and said, "Indeed, I said to myself, 'He will surely come out to me, and stand and call on the name of the Lord his God, and wave his hand over the place, and heal the leprosy.' Are not the Abanah and the Pharpar, the rivers of Damascus, better than all the waters of Israel?

*Could I not wash in them and be clean?" So he
turned and went away in a rage. (2 Kings 5:11-
12)*

You can sense Naaman's anger at such a humiliating
order. He was a man of power, dignity, and honor. Who
was he to take orders, much less orders that would
degrade a man of his prominence? The prophet did not
even come out to meet him and work his "magic" as
Naaman supposed he would. Now he—he of all people
in the world!—is to submit himself to the orders of a
man who pays him no respect and plunge into a
humble, ugly, muddy river. Naaman's complaint is
much like ours: "I have too much pride for that!"

More than anything else, pride and arrogance will keep
us from the full healing and delivering work that our
salvation intends for our lives. Namaan refused to
submit himself to the humility of the waters of the
Jordan River, insisting there were much more dignified
means of healing for such a great man.

Pride tells us that we can make God's life happen for
ourselves. Pride tells us that we are more spiritually
mature than we actually are. Pride keeps us tied down
to sin and the sickness it causes because pride never
allows us to admit that we are not as strong as we hope
we are. Pride hides sin; it does not get it out in the open
where it can be dealt with. The reality is that while
Namaan refused to humble himself and obey the Word
of the Lord, he remained in his sickness and bondage.

There was a time in my life where I was bound in a certain sin. I knew it was wrong, and I did my best to continually give it to Jesus. With all sincerity, I can say that there was no part of my spiritual man that desired this sin but my fleshly man did. Yet the root of this sin was my own pride. Pride allowed for an unlocked door in my soul through which the devil could enter and keep me bound. I would think, "It's okay; I am mature enough to handle a little bit of this sin." What a prideful self-delusion! I would also have the thought, "God will forgive me...I won't go to hell for this."

Listen to me! The question is not God's ability to forgive us, for He always forgives those who come in true repentance. What bothers God is that when we make room for sin, we are destroying ourselves. We are undoing the very process for which He saved us! Forgiveness is not the issue, the undoing of our souls is. When sin is introduced into our lives, there is forgiveness, but there are also consequences that bring brokenness, pain, and bondage.

The reality is that we cannot purify and "fix" ourselves through our nice ideas, good works, and certainly not through our prideful self-sufficiency. All other places and methods that God has not indicated for our purification, the worldly methods, self-help books, and inspirational ideas—and even our own sense of self-sufficiency—look and sound wonderful, but they lack power. Like Namaan preferring to bathe in the rivers in

Syria, our own desires and methods cannot result in our healing, deliverance, or cleansing. Baptism works because it is the place God has told us to go for our deliverance. It is the place of humility, obedience, submission, cleansing, deliverance, and healing.

Where are the places in your life that you have not yet submitted to God even if you have been saved for many years? What are the areas where you keep doors open to spiritual bondage, physical sickness, or the consequences of your sin that keep breaking your life? If you have never been baptized, submit to the waters in humility and be free. If you have been baptized, then I want to encourage you to seek out a pastor or a trusted, spiritually mature friend and confess your sin and bondage. James 5:16 tells us the path to healing: *"Confess your trespasses to one another, and pray for one another, that you may be healed..."* Baptism is a step of humility and obedience, but can you think of a step that requires even ***more*** humility and obedience than confessing your sins out loud?! Confession leads to deliverance and healing.

Participation

Just as there is a link between purity of heart and revelation of God, there is also a link between the purification Jesus gives us and our participation in His life and work. One of the most potent metaphors in Scriptures for baptism is in the Tabernacle that God instructed Moses to build. Before a priest could go into the Tabernacle itself and minister to the Lord, the priest was required to go through three stations in the temple courtyard before he was acceptable to minister to the Lord. We will deal with the third area later on.

The first area was the Bronze Altar where the sacrifices for sin were offered. These represent the ultimate sacrifice that Jesus made for our sins on the cross. The second station was a large bronze washing bowl, the Laver, in which the priests needed to bathe themselves. *After* making the sacrifice for sin, the priests had to wash themselves and be purified from their sin to be able to minister to the Lord! Along with the Laver, the priests had to wear special clothes that were made specifically to minister to the Lord and to be used only for that purpose. They were forgiven, purified, and changed in their clothing—everything about them had been cleansed to minister to the Lord! It amazes me that such a potent picture of baptism was given by the Lord in the symbolism of the first Tabernacle! God's plan of salvation and His principles for living rightly in His Kingdom have not changed from the Old Testament to the New Testament.

Likewise, only hours before His crucifixion, Jesus shared the Last Supper with His disciples—the men who would soon carry on the work of the Lord in the world. During this meal, Jesus took a towel and a bowl of water and washed the feet of His disciples. Peter protested saying, *"You shall never wash my feet!"* Jesus simply responded saying, *"If I do not wash you, you have no part in me."* To be part of God's full plan, we must allow Him to wash and prepare us. This washing is in baptism. Baptism is a doorway that allows us entrance into Jesus' full cleansing work and thus into full participation in His life and work.

VI

Baptism
Entrance Into God's Family

The fact that God became a human being is something
that our minds are not fully capable of understanding.
In his book, *Incarnation*, Tom Baker eloquently states
that the potter threw himself on the wheel as the clay,
the composer became a note on the staff of his music,
the painter became the paint on his own canvas. God
became human. How humbling for God and how
ennobling for man.[14] Why would God do such a thing?
We have already spoken of the main reason—to save us
from our slavery to sin and death. But once we are
freed from slavery, a whole new world of possibilities
and promises opens up to us. C.S. Lewis said it like
this: "The Son of God became a man to enable men to
become sons of God."[15] In short, through His death and
resurrection, we can enter into a new Kingdom and be
part of a new family, which carries enormous
implications for us.

We have covered the first two events surrounding Jesus' baptism, those being the fulfillment of all righteousness and the heavens opening. The third event in Jesus' baptism that occurred is a voice from heaven saying, *"This is my beloved Son, in whom I am well pleased"* (Matthew 3:17).

These words spoken to Jesus were much more that what we would see as a proud dad at his child's soccer game screaming, "That's my boy!" after he scored a goal. Rather, these were words declaring Jesus' **divine position** as God incarnate, His affirming **acceptance as a human being,** and the perfect sacrifice for the world. In fact, it was John the Baptist who, moments before Jesus' baptism, declared, *"Behold! The Lamb of God who takes away the sins of the world!"* (John 1:29). This declaration was the summation of Jesus' divinity and humanity—God Himself, wrapped in humanity, had come to be humanity's ransom.

Born Again

Jesus being God-in-the-flesh, along with the fact that He was accepted as both human and divine, carries enormous significance for us. Jesus' humanity united the human race again with the divine—only One who was both man and God could do such a thing for us. As we have already seen, baptism, which is a representation of our salvation, is also the symbol of our union with Christ Jesus. Jesus Himself instructs us in John 3:5, *"Most assuredly, I say to you, unless one is born of water and the Spirit, he cannot enter the kingdom of God."* Just as we were born physically through our parents and born into a specific family, we must be born of both "water and spirit" to enter into a new Kingdom and a new family. In Jesus Christ, we receive much more than forgiveness of sin and eternal life—we are being offered a place in the family as children of God!

Galatians 3:26-27 says, *"For you are all sons of God through faith in Christ Jesus. For as many of you as were baptized into Christ have put on Christ."* The Apostle Paul continues in Ephesians 4:4-6:

There is one body and one Spirit, just as you were called in one hope of your calling; one Lord, one faith, one baptism; one God and Father of all, who is above all, and through all, and in you all.

During the rest of this chapter, we will examine what God wants to do in and through us because of our status as part of His family, which has eternal ramifications.

A Family Covenant

Throughout Scripture, God establishes seven different covenants with His people. In the Ancient Near East, when a covenant was to be made, the ceremony was literally called "cutting a covenant." A specific ceremony was performed with obligatory elements such as blood sacrifices, exchange of weapons, clothes, and, sometimes, children. Gifts were also given, blessings and curses were declared, and a ceremonial covenant meal was eaten. While these were the most common elements, some covenants included other practices. It is a fascinating study to see how God, in Jesus Christ, fulfilled all the elements of the "cutting of a covenant" with us as His people.

God's blood-covenant with Israel was established on Mount Sinai in Exodus 19-24. As mentioned earlier in this book, marriage, like baptism, is a symbol of something much deeper. The covenant God made with Israel on Mount Sinai is also viewed as a marriage covenant between God and His people. Marriage is a covenant of faithfulness, but it is also the beginning of a new family.

The covenant God made with us in Jesus Christ is called "The New Covenant." As a matter of fact, this is what the "Old Testament" and "New Testament" literally mean—the old and the new covenants. No covenant was complete without the blood sacrifice. The sacrifice represented the gravity of the partnership between the two parties involved. In the Old Covenant in the Bible, there were animal sacrifices that were continually made to God in worship. In the "cutting" of the New Covenant, Jesus established this with the sacrifice of His own body on the cross with His own blood sealing the covenant! The cutting of this New Covenant means that we are allied with God in a binding treaty, and we are literally in His "blood" line as His family.

The New Covenant means many things for us, one of which is the family covenant. Though a detailed study of all the covenant elements would be worthwhile, I want to focus specifically on two of them here: the exchange of children and of clothes.

In order to enter into this covenant, an exchange of lives is necessary. God, in Jesus, gave His life for us in order to activate this covenant. We must also reciprocate for the covenant to be valid. With Jesus, we have both died and risen again. When we do this through baptism, we are entering into all that is new along with Jesus—Jesus the sacrifice, Jesus the man, Jesus the first raised from the dead, Jesus our brother—Jesus our family (see Hebrews 2:11-17). In effect, when we are baptized, God is saying, ***"In giving my Son for you, I will take you as my child."***

In this way, baptism is this exchange—it is a form of giving. In Luke 6:38, Jesus said, *"Give, and it will be given to you: good measure, pressed down, shaken together, and running over will be put into your bosom. For with the same measure that you use, it will be measured back to you."* In baptism, and the covenant God made with us, He asks us to give all to Him and, in exchange, He gives all of Himself to us. It is as if God is saying, ***"Give me all that you have***

been with all your failures, sins, and shortcomings, and I will give back to you all of the purity, forgiveness, and love that I am!" When we give all of ourselves to God, He gives us back "good measure, pressed down, shaken together, and running over." We have an amazing abundance when we give ourselves to Him! Even though it may appear that God gets the losing end of the covenant, He still comes out the winner because He has us back as we are His most valued treasures!

Also in the covenant-making ceremony, an exchange of clothing transpires. The covenant partners exchange clothes with each other to fuse their identities together. If anyone were to see one of the covenant partners in public, one covenant partner would be mistaken for the other. The exchange of clothing was not meant to be a loss of identity, rather a symbol of an unbreakable covenant uniting the two parties. They were to be so united from this covenant that, in essence, "you are me, and I am you."

As it pertains to the New Covenant God established with us in Jesus, there too, was an exchange of clothing. Jesus Christ was clothed in glory. As the second member of the eternal Godhead, He became flesh and literally clothed Himself with human skin. We, however, were clothed with every type of destructive sin. 2 Corinthians 5:21 tells us that *"God made Him who knew no sin to become sin for us so that in Him we might become the righteousness of*

God." Jesus clothed Himself not just in flesh but with our sins as well. In exchange, we are clothed with the righteousness of Christ Jesus. In Ephesians 4:22-24, the Apostle Paul further clarifies this truth:

...put off, concerning your former conduct, the old man which grows corrupt according to the deceitful lusts, and be renewed in the spirit of your mind, and that you put on the new man which was created according to God, in true righteousness and holiness.

In this exchange, God also gives us new clothes to wear. Our identity has been united to Jesus. Isaiah 61:10 explains, *"I will greatly rejoice in the Lord, my soul shall be joyful in my God; for He has clothed me with the **garments of salvation**, He has covered me with the robe of righteousness..."* When we walk down the street, we want people to confuse us with Jesus! They will see that there is something different about us that distinguishes us from others. Baptism is not something that happens once and then it is over. It is entering into a covenant, a new family, with new clothes and a new way of living.

Transformation

When people see us, we want them to see Jesus. But this is more than a mixing of identities; through baptism, God wants to work a complete transformation in our entire being. We need to look like Jesus in every way possible; in the way He talks, acts, and thinks.

In chapter four, we introduced the Greek word "baptidzo." Baptizdo means to drown, sink, or perish. But there is another aspect to this word which is "to dye clothing." When an article of clothing is dipped, or sunk, into the color, the material remains the same. If it is wool or cotton, it remains wool or cotton, but **all** the material is transformed in its appearance as it is sunk into the dye.

Likewise, an eternal transformation is associated with baptism. For example, when cucumber is submerged in a vinegar solution, it becomes a pickle. Over time, the pickling solution completely penetrates the cucumber. The flavor, the appearance, the feeling, and **even the use of it** have all changed, though it still remains a cucumber, it is a transformed cucumber!

When I was in the fourth grade, I had a project to make for history class. I had to make a bow and arrows. I had to find a way to bend the tree branch and make it flexible enough to make it into a bow. I did it by soaking it in water for a few days until it was completely saturated. After some time, it was very easy to transform it into the desired shape. Submerging the wood in water caused its pliability and thus, its transformation. The essence of the wood remained the same, but it was able to be formed into an instrument of more effective use. In his book _Mere Christianity_, C.S. Lewis likewise correlates the concept of transformation with salvation:

People often think of Christian morality as a kind of bargain in which God says, 'If you keep a lot of rules I'll reward you, and if you don't I'll do the other thing.' I do not think that is the best way of looking at it. I would much rather say that every time you make a choice you are turning the central part of you, the part of you that chooses, into something a little different from what it was before. And taking your life as a whole, with all your innumerable choices, all your life long you are slowly turning this central thing either into a heavenly creature or into a hellish creature: either into a creature that is in harmony with God, and with other creatures, and with itself, or else into one that is in a state of war and hatred with God, and with its fellow-creatures, and with itself. To be the one kind of creature is heaven: that is, it is joy and peace and knowledge and power. To be the other means madness, horror , idiocy, rage, impotence, and eternal loneliness. Each of us at each moment is progressing to the one state or the other.[16]

In baptism, God transforms our entire being. Like the article of clothing, it remains the same material, but everything about it has changed. In baptism, we remain the same in our being, but everything about our nature has changed to be like Jesus—in reality, we are

becoming more like the real "us"—the people God
wanted us to be from the very beginning. Like the
pickle, our essence, flavor, and the way God uses us has
changed. Like with the bow and arrows, our lives in
baptism become flexible in His hands so that He can
form us for His maximum usage. C.S. Lewis continues
by asserting the following:

*And now we begin to see what it is that the
New Testament is always talking about. It
talks about Christians 'being born again'; it
talks about them 'putting on Christ'; about
Christ 'being formed in us'; about our coming
to 'have the mind of Christ'. Put right out of
your head the idea that these are only fancy
ways of saying that Christians are to read
what Christ said and try to carry it out— as a
man may read what Plato or Marx said and
try to carry it out. They mean something much
more than that. They mean that a real Person,
Christ, here and now, in that very room where
you are saying your prayers, is doing things to
you. It is not a question of a good man who
died two thousand years ago. It is a living
Man, still as much a man as you, and still as
much God as He was when He created the
world, really coming and interfering with your
very self; killing the old natural self in you and
replacing it with the kind of self He has. At
first, only for moments. Then for longer
periods. Finally, if all goes well, turning you*

*permanently into a different sort of thing; into
a new little Christ, a being which, in its own
small way, has the same kind of life as God;
which shares in His power, joy, knowledge and
eternity.*[17]

All of us need our lives changed in the waters of
baptism because the former ways of living are not
compatible with whom God is. Living in our past sins
and habits does not measure up with the life, the
Kingdom, and the family that God is giving to us. The
Christian life is much more than a religion or a simple
system of belief: It is a dynamic relationship with Jesus
Christ and a transformation of our lives to become like
Him, thereby, enabling us to live the life that He
designed for us and carry out the work He has in store
for us.

As recorded in Ephesians 2:10, *"...we are His
workmanship, created in Christ Jesus for good works,
which God prepared beforehand that we should walk
in them."* We are not saved **by** good works, but we are
saved **for** good works! God has something very special
for our lives to accomplish, and He wants to transform
us so that we accomplish it!

The Purpose of the New Family
Every family has a different identity and calling. My
family is very different from my brother's in spite of the
fact that we come from the same family. He married a
blonde girl, and since he was blonde as a child, they

have four kids that are shockingly blonde—they look like four dandelions! I, on the other hand, married a Mexican girl (a beautiful Tapatía from Guadalajara! #blessed) and our four children are bilingual and a beautiful mix of Caucasian and Mexican. We are close families, but at the same time very different. Still there are other families both my brother and I know that have completely different mentalities, interests, habits, methods of child-rearing, and sense of calling and identity. Every family, just like every person, is unique and God's family is no different.

When we come into God's family through salvation, we come into a family that is already established with God as our Father. This new family has a way of life that is very different from the ways our natural families live. However, the calling of this family needs to be realized, and baptism is a step of obedience that prepares us to function in this family. We read in the last chapter that the Israelite priests had to wash themselves in the Laver before ministering in the Tabernacle to the Lord in preparation to serve Him. As we come into God's family, we inherit the calling our Father has placed on us—and this calling is that every member is a priest. Look at what Peter says concerning our priesthood:

But you are a chosen generation, a royal priesthood, a holy nation, His own special people, that you may proclaim the praises of Him who called you out of darkness into His marvelous light; who once were not a people

but are now the people of God, who had not
obtained mercy but now have obtained mercy.
(1 Peter 2:9-10)

While it is unnecessary to reiterate, we need to understand that we have the blessing of being a part of God's family. There is a calling and job as part of this family to function in authority as His children.

Part of this family-responsibility is to be continually interconnected with our family of faith since we are all part of one another. Because God has a covenant with us in Christ, then there is also a covenant in Christ one with another. Many sincere people who love Jesus believe that their personal knowledge of God's Word, their spiritual maturity, or wisdom is sufficient. Yet, at the same time, there appears to be a total disregard to live life as the family of God. This is an erroneous way of thinking. Psalm 68:6 says that God *"sets the solitary in families."* When we are not part of each other, we deprive ourselves of what others have to offer, and we deprive others of the good gifts, talents, and love we have to offer. Just as we do not abandon our earthly families, neither should we neglect our spiritual family.

Even as God declared of Jesus at His baptism that He was His Son and He was pleased with Him, when we are brought into God's family, as with Jesus, it is as if there is a declaration from God to our divine position as His children—almost like a birth certificate! And as God also affirmed Jesus' divine position as His Son and confirmed the acceptance of Jesus' humanity, God also affirms us as His people and confirms our "fulfilling all righteousness" in doing what is good, right, and just. And remember one more thing: God is pleased with you!

VII

The Baptism of Jesus

John 4:2 reveals that Jesus did not baptize with water, but it was His disciples who baptized people. Have you ever wondered why Jesus did not baptize? He clearly thought it important or He Himself would not have been baptized nor commanded all believers to submit to it. We see the answer in Luke 3:16:

*John [the Baptist] answered, saying to all, "I indeed baptize you with water; but One mightier than I is coming, whose sandal strap I am not worthy to loose. He will baptize you with the **Holy Spirit** and **fire**.*

Jesus did not baptize with water because He had a different baptism to give us. I will deal more with the baptism with the Holy Spirit in chapter 8. But here it is necessary to bring into focus the baptism that Jesus

Himself came to bring us. Up to this point we have spoken mainly about baptism in water, but Jesus came to baptize us with the Holy Spirit and with fire.

A Baptism of Holiness

Have you ever wondered why the Holy Spirit is called the "HOLY" Spirit? Why not the "powerful" Spirit? Or the "good" Spirit? Or some other adjective that would fit His miraculous, transformative power? In talking about the baptism with the Holy Spirit and with fire, it would be remiss to not talk about the holy nature of the Holy Spirit—or the "Spirit of Holiness."

Holiness is often misunderstood. It is many times thought of in terms of a God who is unreachable, angry, and so "holy" that He is ready to smash us to bits the moment we sin. So holiness becomes a word of terror for many people who imagine God to be both isolated from us and ready to commit us to an eternity in Hell.

The term "holiness" also gets a bad rap from some people who, I am sure, are well meaning and sincere in their love for God, who, instead of an attitude of humility, love, and patience, carry an air of superiority, prudishness, or hyper-religiosity that turns up its nose at everything they happen to disapprove of. Unfortunately, both you and I have known people like this, but let me emphatically state that holiness has nothing to do with such attitudes or actions. That is pride!

The continual act of the Holy Spirit aiding the recovery of God's image in our lives is the picture of God's holiness in action. Holiness has to do with completeness. In fact, the etymology of the English word "holy" is derived from the Old English *halig* which means "whole." Simply put, holiness is everything that is good, healthy, and pure. Holiness has been defined by some as "the health of God." Nothing that is whole—holy—is fractured, broken, profane, impure, or for common use.

God Himself is holy. In both Isaiah 6 and Revelation 4 we are given a window into Heaven and the ongoing worship around the throne of God. The creatures around the throne do not cease to proclaim the essence of God's character in their cries of adoration as they shout, "Holy, holy, holy!" God's holiness is the source of life and the goodness and health He created it to be.

In seeing the eternal throne room of God and the **worship** of His character of holiness, we first see the holiness of God **revealed** in Scripture through His goodness in creation. While God was creating the world, seven times He looked at His work and declared that it was "good." The full creative work of God in creation reveals the goodness environment full of beauty and provision in which He placed humankind.[18]

His goodness is also revealed in His original intent with which He created humanity: He created us to participate with Him in every aspect of His life, work, and rulership, and to enjoy relationship one with another. God's holiness is His character, and this holiness is expressed through His acts of goodness toward His creation and humanity. It is, and has always been, God's intention to do good to you—because **holy** is who He **is** and **goodness** is what He **does**. He cannot do anything else but work goodness—even when we do not fully understand what God is doing in a given moment or circumstance. In fact, the prophet Jeremiah announced God's judgment upon the people of Israel for their persistent, unrepentant idolatry. Their punishment was a 70-years long banishment from the land of Israel in Babylonia. Yet even in the midst of this severe punishment, God speaks to them saying, *"For I know the thoughts that I think toward you, says the Lord, thoughts of peace and not of evil, to give you a future and a hope"* (Jeremiah 29:11).

Even in punishment, God says that He is intending good for them! God's severity is not to humiliate or demoralize people, but it is for the purpose of forging His character of holiness in us. God **cannot** work brokenness into people because His nature and character are holy, and His holiness is exemplified through wholeness, purity, and health. Anything that is unhealthy in us has to be transformed when brought into His holiness.

Baptism into God's holiness is the purpose of our salvation. We are not saved for the sole purpose of getting to Heaven. Those of us who have received Jesus

Christ as our Lord and Savior and have repented of our sins will go to Heaven one day—but that is not the expressed reason for which we were saved. We were saved to recover all of God's original purpose for our lives that was lost because of our rebellion. We are saved to be transformed again into the very image of God in which we were originally created but which was destroyed in us through sin. Romans 8:29 tells us this very thing: *"For whom He foreknew, He also predestined to be conformed to the image of His Son..."* We were saved to come back into the holiness—the wholeness and health—of God.

Holy Fire and Deliverance

The ministry of Moses is an archetype of the ministry of Jesus. Moses delivered the people of Israel from slavery as Christ delivered us from sin. The similarities of their lives and ministries are astonishing, and there are some comparisons between the two that need to be made in regards to the baptism of holy fire as God's delivering power in our lives.

The Hebrew word *qodesh* is the root word for *holy*. The first time this word appears is in Genesis 2:3 where God makes the seventh and final day of creation holy. This sanctification represented the perfect Creation, holy and at rest.[19] After the fall of humanity into sin which unleashed the brokenness—unholiness—over the earth as a result, we see none of God's holiness (*qodesh*) in Hebrew Scripture until Exodus 3:5 when God appears to Moses out of the burning bush. When

Moses turns aside and comes near to see the wonder of a bush that is engulfed with flames yet not consumed by them, the Lord speaks to him saying, *"Do not draw near this place. Take your sandals off your feet, for the place where you stand is holy ground."* **The holiness of God was revealed to Moses out of the fire at the precise moment God appointed for the deliverance of His people from their bondage in Egypt.**

The revelation of God's holiness is set against the story of a nation, set aside by God for His special purpose, enslaved and living in everything less than what God created them to be. Yet God's holiness will manifest itself in goodness by coming to set His people free from the brokenness of their bondage. The manifestation of God's holiness through His goodness comes in three different signs given to Moses. These three signs give deep insight into the power of God's holy work in our lives.

The first sign was the burning bush itself. The fire of God was the sign of the very real closeness of His presence. God draws near to the oppressed and His presence has the power to deliver from bondage. The burning bush is the sign that deliverance has come.

The second and third signs given to Moses were for those elders of Israel who would not believe God had actually sent Moses. These signs were to help the elders believe, but they were far from simply magic tricks—

they were a symbol of what God intended to do with the people He was about to save. For the second sign, God commanded Moses to throw down his staff so it would become a serpent. I don't know about you, but if I saw that, I would have run the other way—snakes freak me out! But God commanded Moses to grab the snake by the tail, and when he did, the snake turned back into a staff.

Throughout Scripture, the snake is an obvious reference to satanic powers. Moses was about to go to Egypt where an evil king who served demon idols was oppressing God's people. This sign of the Moses' staff turning into a snake, and then Moses' ability to take the snake back into his hand, is one of God granting authority over ruling, malevolent powers in Egypt. God's holiness has come to break every impure, ungodly, enslaving power of hell over our lives and to give us the authority to live in freedom. Like Moses, it is for this expressed purpose Jesus came. 1 John 3:8 tells us *"...For this purpose the Son of God was manifested, that He might destroy the works of the devil."*

When Jesus sent His disciples out to minister the Gospel of the Kingdom, He told them, *"I give you the authority to trample on serpents and scorpions, and over all the power of the enemy, and nothing shall by any means hurt you"* (Luke 10:19). This same authority that Moses experienced and that Jesus has and shared with His disciples is available to us!

For the third sign, God told Moses to put his hand in his robe. Upon doing so, Moses' hand became white with leprosy. When instructed to put his hand back in his robe, the hand was made clean. What an amazing picture of God's holiness! God has come to take people who are infected with the stink of death and sin, and make them fully clean! The holiness of God's character and the subsequent manifestation of His goodness brought the people close to His presence, delivered them from demonic bondage, and cleansed them for the Lord's use.

We see the similarity of God's holiness and goodness at work in Jesus' ministry. If I were asked to describe Jesus' earthly ministry, I would most likely describe it as powerful, delivering, Spirit-filled, or miraculous. Yet in Acts 10:38, the Apostle Peter describes it somewhat differently: *"God anointed Jesus of Nazareth with the Holy Spirit and with power, who went about **doing good** and healing all who were oppressed by the devil, for God was with Him."* Did you get that? Jesus' miraculous ministry of deliverance is described as *"doing good!"*

During Jesus' ministry, He encountered the unholy, unclean brokenness of humanity in all of its filth. Jesus, in the first few chapters of Mark's gospel, encountered an *unclean*, demonic spirit, a man with leprosy, (an *unclean* skin disease), a woman with a flow of blood, (an *unclean* discharge), and a dead girl (death being the most *unclean* of all according to the Law of Moses). In each and every case, Jesus, the Man who was filled with the Spirit of God's Holiness, does not become unclean through His contact with these people, rather these people become clean through contact with His holiness![20] Holy is God's character, and that character is manifest through His acts of goodness in delivering people from their bondage and uncleanness. Later, Jesus, in Mark 16:15-18, turns around and tells His disciples to go and do the exact same thing for others:

And He said to them, "Go into all the world and preach the gospel to every creature. He who believes and is baptized will be saved; but he who does not believe will be condemned. And these signs will follow those who believe: In My name they will cast out demons; they will speak with new tongues; they will take up serpents; and if they drink anything deadly, it will by no means hurt them; they will lay hands on the sick, and they will recover.

Holiness is embedded in the very essence and works of God. We see in Moses and the Apostles, that upon their encounters with the holiness of God's Spirit, ***His power is released to them for works of power and redemption that begin to move unclean/unholy and bound people back toward what God's intention for them always was.*** The Baptism with the Holy Spirit is the outworking of God's holiness for the restoration of people. *Repentance* enacts salvation, but *holiness* is salvation in action!

A Baptism of Holy Fire

Just as there is a misconception concerning the holiness of God, there is an equal misconception regarding the baptism Jesus gives with fire. Baptism with fire is commonly understood to be the same as the baptism with the Holy Spirit, which is God's supernatural power for ministry, which restores people back to wholeness. However, fire in the Scriptures is not a symbol of God's power but rather of His holiness.

The first time fire is mentioned in the Bible is the flaming sword of the Cherubim who guarded the way to the Tree of Life so that Adam and Eve could not eat of it. In other words, the fire and the sword disallowed them entrance into the presence of God because of their sin. The next context fire is presented to us in the Bible is the context of God destroying Sodom and Gomorrah, the two cities that had become morally depraved and vile in every sense of the word.

Throughout the Scriptures, fire is used by God to burn up sacrifices, which carried the sins of the people. Fire is also used to consume falsehood and fruitlessness in God's people. Several times the Bible describes God's response to sin and rebellion as His anger being kindled. There is also eternal hell fire awaiting those who will not repent of their sins. Deuteronomy 4:24, which is repeated in Hebrews 12:29, says, *"For the*

Lord your God is a consuming fire, a jealous God."

God originally revealed His holiness through His goodness. How is it, then, that God's holiness is so often revealed through fire—and terrifying images of consuming fire? How are the fires of Sodom and Gomorrah or the fires of hell good? How could the God, who is a "consuming fire," be good? Yet, these are not the only times God reveals His holiness in fire.

God revealed His fire in the burning bush to Moses; in the pillar of cloud and fire to lead His people after their deliverance from Egypt; on Mt. Sinai when He established Israel as His covenant people; in Malachi's prophecy of the refining work of the Messiah; and in the tongues of fire that came upon believers at coming of the Holy Spirit on the day of Pentecost.

If we carefully examine how God uses fire to reveal Himself in holiness, we will see that His fire is principally used for two purposes: to devour or to deliver. The fire of God's holiness is the result of our sin—not of God's anger. Since God's holiness is His health, purity, and wholeness, then anything that is not within His character is going to meet with His fire. In other words, since God is pure and we are stained with sin, there is going to be a consequence. Since God is whole and we are broken, there is going to be a reaction.

The image of fire is employed because fire can consume

anything and everything—God's fire even consumed the water poured over the prophet Elijah's sacrifice! Proverbs 30:16 tells us that fire is never satiated—it will burn until there is nothing left to burn.

Wherever there exists something in God's good creation that does not reflect His goodness or holiness, it is out of line with God's natural order. Disaster, sickness, evil, hatred, idolatry, immorality, relational dysfunction, emotional and mental disorders, and death are all outside the created order of God's holiness. And yet we consider that all the brokenness of life we have experienced is normal. We say things like, "That's life," or "Qué será será." But what we experience is actually abnormal—it was never meant to be this way. God's fire burns away the abnormalities of sin and death to bring everything back in line with His original order.

God's fire devours or delivers—but His fire is the result of the contact holiness has with brokenness. God's fire will devour the brokenness and sin of every person on earth. Whether the fire devours a person or delivers him/her; punishes or purifies him/her, depends on each person's response to God's holiness and salvation in Jesus Christ. If we repent of our sins, God's fire will purify our lives, consume the brokenness and sin, and restore His order in our lives. If we refuse Him and tenaciously hold on to our sin, then the fire of hell awaits, not because God hates people, but because sin *must* be consumed and those who hold to it will be consumed along with it.

John the Baptist said that Jesus will baptize us with the Holy Spirit and fire. Listen to how The Message translates these words in Luke 3:16-17:

I'm baptizing you here in the river. The main character in this drama, to whom I'm a mere stagehand, will ignite the kingdom life, a fire, the Holy Spirit within you, changing you from the inside out. He's going to clean house—make a clean sweep of your lives; place everything true in its proper place before God; everything false he'll put out with the trash to be burned.[21]

Set Apart

The Tabernacle, and later the Temple, that was built for the dwelling place of God among His people, was a place of complete holiness. Every part of the Tabernacle was to be sanctified with the blood of a sacrifice to eradicate any impurity or unholiness that might have touched it. This was to be the place where the holy God would be able to dwell with an unholy people. The priests themselves, their garments, and all the specialized tools used for ministry in the Tabernacle were made holy for their dedicated use. In its essence and function, the Tabernacle was the place of total holiness where God's holy presence could find a place to be with His people.

In Ezekiel 43:12, God gives the prophet a vision of the

new Temple that is going to be built and He says, *"And this is the basic law of the Temple: absolute holiness!"* (NLT). In this we see yet another aspect of God's holiness: someone or something that is set apart for specific use by God. In 1 Corinthians 3:16 and 6:19, twice we are told that **we** are the Temple of the Holy Spirit. We, then, are to live in absolute holiness. We are to live set apart for God's specific purposes.

Baptism and the Crucible

The baptism with fire is the crucible in which God forges His people. The process of God's holiness is making us more like Him everyday—making our hearts an acceptable Temple for His Spirit to dwell in. Yet in John the Baptist's words that Jesus would baptize with the Holy Spirit and fire, and in the results of Jesus' baptism through which the Holy Spirit endued Him with power, the baptism Jesus pours out on us indicates both the filling with supernatural power as well as the fire of the purification of the soul; the crucible in which God forges the heart and character of His people.

The baptism with the power of the Holy Spirit for supernatural ministry was not meant to be the zenith of our faith. It is not a gold medal of something we have achieved or to be boasted in as if God smiles upon us a little bit more than He does on other believers. Baptism with the Holy Spirit's power is a tool to be used to live as Jesus lived and to minister beyond our natural capacities, just as He ministered. There are many who focus on the momentary manifestations of power. However, the zenith of our faith is not in power. Nor does the greatest miracle happen in the electrifying experience of an encounter with God—these things are God's means to the end of His holiness being formed in us. The greatest and most difficult miracle is in the transformation of a deformed soul into a Christ-like person.

Samson is a prime example of a man with ***charisma*** of the Spirit without the ***character*** of holiness; one who was ***doing*** miracles without ***being*** like God. Arguably the most famous of Israel's Judges, Samson was endued with supernatural physical abilities. If ever there was a formidable man of God to whom one could point to the specific, overpowering, charismatic works of miracle power...it was Samson. But Samson also ran after prostitutes and continually disobeyed God's commands. He was powerful and did amazing things, but at the end of the day, he was self-indulgent, undisciplined, and disobedient, and his works died along with him.

Jesus Himself speaks to the issue of power without character and obedience in Matthew 7:21-23:

Not everyone who says to Me, "Lord, Lord," shall enter the kingdom of heaven, but he who does the will of My Father in heaven. Many will say to Me in that day, "Lord, Lord, have we not prophesied in Your name, cast out

demons in Your name, and done many
wonders in Your name?" And then I will
declare to them, "I never knew you; depart
from Me, you who practice lawlessness!"

The proof of a Christ-like life is not in the works of
power, it is in obedience to the Lord in all things.
Charismatic ministry without the fire-forged character
of God's holiness makes for an immature and shallow
ministry. I prefer a mature, discipled, disciplined
person over one who simply works a miracle.

I will never forget the time I led worship at a
conference for children's workers. I was a children's
pastor at my church, and our church gave a special,
one-day seminar for people who ministered to children.
During the closing session, we had a time of ministry,
and there were several pastors who were prepared to
pray for people. There was a specific lady praying, and
everyone this woman prayed for fell down to the
ground. I was close enough to see what was really
happening. She was pushing people over and grabbing
and twisting their arms to "help" them fall down.

I was incensed. Not only was I upset at such
manipulative, fleshly ministry practices, but also that
the line of people waiting for her to pray for them was
by far the longest. Sincere people who desperately
wanted a touch from Father God were lining up to be
prayed for by an immature person. I do not doubt her
or anyone else's sincerity in their love for Jesus, but I

do doubt the maturity of the ministry. When the focus is all about the visible manifestation of the Spirit, the deeper character of the Spirit is often overlooked.

The baptism with fire is the process of refining and purifying that forms God's character in us. In His baptism, Jesus received the power of the Holy Spirit for miraculous, charismatic ministry. Yet we also see the forging of Jesus' character. Luke 2:51 tells us that Jesus was obedient to His parents. Hebrews 5:8 further describes Jesus' formation, *"He learned obedience by the things which He suffered."* Even after receiving power from the Holy Spirit at His baptism, Jesus did not immediately begin to function in this power. Rather, the Holy Spirit took Him out into the desert for forty days to be tested by the devil.

Jesus Himself, filled with power, still had to go through the crucible of character formation. God was interested not in simply a man who could perform the miraculous, but One whom He could trust to be obedient and represent His character to the world. Yet in Jesus' own words, He declares that *"He who has seen Me has seen the Father...Believe Me that I am in the Father and the Father in Me, or else believe Me for the sake of the works themselves."* (John 14:9 and 11). Jesus makes reference to, and Himself is, a convergence of both the **character** of the Father in Him and the **charisma** (miracles) that was worked through Him. ***God wants <u>both</u> from His people.***

Baptized in the Name of Jesus

As we are baptized into the Name of Jesus (remember we are to be baptized in the Name of the Father, **the Son**, and the Holy Spirit), we are sharing in the dimension of life and authority of who Jesus is and what He provides to His people. The reason for our salvation is not simply to go to heaven, but to reclaim in Jesus Christ all of God's purpose and authority that was lost due to sin's slavery over our lives. As we are baptized in His name, we begin to live into the full power of His name. Living the life of a disciple in the power of the name of Jesus permits us to walk in the spiritual dimensions of 1) salvation for our spirits, 2) healing for our souls and bodies, and 3) authority to extend Jesus' life and power through our own lives.

Acts chapter three recounts the first miracle of healing in the Early Church. Peter and John entered the Temple when they saw a man begging by the entrance who had been lame for more than forty years. The man expected to receive some money from the two Apostles. But instead Peter, full of the Holy Spirit, said, *"Silver and gold I do not have, but what I do have I give to you:* **In the name of Jesus Christ** *of Nazareth, rise up and walk!"* The miracle provided an opportunity for Peter to preach the Gospel of Jesus Christ in the Temple compound and many were saved.

Faith in the Name of Jesus is what allows us to walk in such spiritual authority. During Peter's preaching, in Acts 3:16 he says these words, *"And His name, through faith in His name, has made this man strong, whom you see and know. Yes, the faith which comes through Him has given him this perfect soundness in the presence of you all."*

The power and authority in the Name of Jesus is due to His victory over satan on the Cross. In His death and resurrection—which we take part of in baptism—Jesus secured for all of humanity the very purposes of God for our lives which had been lost. Now, baptized in His Name, with faith and the Holy Spirit, we go forward in the same power and authority in which Jesus Himself functioned. Take a moment to read through these few Scriptures that outline the power and authority of the Name of Jesus:

Colossians 2:13-15, *"And you, being dead in your trespasses and the uncircumcision of your flesh, He has made alive together with Him, having forgiven you all trespasses, having wiped out the handwriting of requirements that was against us, which was contrary to us. And He has taken it out of the way, having nailed it to the cross. **Having disarmed principalities and powers, He made a public spectacle of them, triumphing over them in it** [the cross]."*

Philippians 2:8-11, *"And being found in appearance as a man, He humbled Himself and became obedient to the point of death, even* *the death of the cross. **Therefore God also has highly exalted Him and given Him the name which is above every name**, that at the name of Jesus every knee should bow, of those in heaven, and of those on earth, and of those under the earth, and that every tongue should confess that Jesus Christ is Lord, to the glory of God the Father."*

*Acts 4:12, "Nor is there salvation in any other, **for there is no other name** under heaven given among men by which we must be saved."*

*Mark 16:17-18, "And these signs will follow those who believe: **In My name** they will cast out demons; they will speak with new tongues; they will take up serpents; and if they drink anything deadly, it will by no means hurt them; they will lay hands on the sick, and they will recover."*

*Matthew 28:18-19, "And Jesus came and spoke to them, saying, "**All authority has been given to Me in heaven and on earth**. Go therefore and make disciples of all the nations, baptizing them in the name of the Father and of the Son and of the Holy Spirit."*

Baptism in the Name of Jesus calibrates our spiritual life to live at the dimensions of life and power that Jesus' Name provides for salvation, healing, and authority. Baptism and faith in the Name of Jesus brings us into all the spiritual benefits God affords us through salvation. As a matter of fact, Romans 8:16-17 tells us that as God's children, we are co-heirs with Jesus! Everything He is and has is readily available to us. Jesus' Name is healing. We see it clearly in this story: faith in the Name of Jesus made this man whole. The Name of Jesus opens the door to spiritual authority and the full recovery of the dominion and governance we were created to possess from the very beginning.

VIII

Baptism
Open Doors To The Supernatural

Our church baptistery's heater was broken on a chilly
March night when my brother and I stepped into the
ice-cold waters to be baptized. Our father, who was an
associate pastor at our church, was going to baptize us.
Both my brother and I, who were respectively twelve
and ten, had greatly anticipated this night, and we were
excited and emotional waiting for our turn to go under
the water. The pastor was praying for the candidates as
we all stood in the water. I couldn't wait for him to
finish praying because I was shivering from the cold
water!

My being there was the result of the very first time God
had ever spoken to me. I will never forget that moment.
I was ten years old. I had not been in prayer. I was not
seeking God at the moment. I was not asking for a sign
or a voice from Heaven. I was simply doing my routine
Saturday morning chores vacuuming my bedroom. I

had never heard God speak before. Incidentally, many people have not heard God's voice speak directly to their heart before, and many times this fact in and of itself becomes an impediment for them hearing God's voice and they become discouraged. However, I have learned that God has no trouble connecting with people whose hearts are willing and open. Be encouraged! Jesus instructed us regarding such things saying, *"Seek and you will find,"* (Matthew 7:7)

As I pushed the vacuum across the bedroom floor, all of a sudden, I heard two words reverberate clearly in my soul, "Get baptized." I instantly knew it was God. It certainly was not any thought of my own, in fact, I had never even considered baptism before that moment. In obedience to the voice of the Lord, I told my parents of my encounter with God and we set a date for my baptism. In this same time frame, God had also been speaking to my brother about being baptized.

A couple weeks later we stood in the baptistry shivering with both cold and anticipation as our dad baptized the first candidates. It was my brother's turn. I watched my dad ask him if he believed in Jesus Christ as his Lord and Savior, and he affirmed it. My dad took Brian under the water and immediately upon rising from the waters, I heard my brother, for the first time in his life, begin to speak in tongues while he praised the Lord. I felt so happy for him! At the same time, I felt a little nervous because I desperately wanted the same thing to happen to me. During the previous week of waiting for my baptism, I was praying very diligently asking God that during my baptism that I would also be filled with the Holy Spirit. I remember sitting in my fifth grade classroom, not paying attention to my lessons, praying under my breath for the baptism of the Holy Spirit.

It was my turn. My dad asked me the same question he had asked my brother, and I also affirmed my love, belief, and commitment to the Lord Jesus Christ. Now, only moments before, a thought occurred to me in my ten-year-old brain. I wondered what would happen under the water if I opened my eyes. Would I see angels? Would I see anything different? Would I see an open heaven while I was underneath the holy waters of baptism? Admittedly, it was not the most mature thought, but give me a little space—I was ten! Let me assure you, that when you open your eyes under the baptismal waters, nothing looks different.

Prior to our baptism, we were instructed not to simply rise from the water and make a beeline for the changing room. We were to wait, lift our hands, and begin to praise the Lord and expect God to meet us there in a powerful way...and He did. As I came up from the water, I lifted my hands and simply said, "I praise you, Lord..." when I was immediately baptized in the power of the Holy Spirit and began to speak in tongues. It was one of the most powerful experiences of my life. I stood there for a long time praising God in an unlearned tongue just as Jesus' disciples did in Acts 2.

Though many people do not experience the baptism of the Holy Spirit in the waters of baptism, it is still an expectation that we can receive the promise of the Father, the Holy Spirit, at the same time we are baptized. It happened to me. It happened to my brother. It has happened to countless others. It also happened to Jesus.

When Jesus submitted Himself to baptism, four things occurred: 1) He fulfilled "all righteousness," 2) the heavens were opened, 3) an affirming voice from heaven was heard, and 4) the Holy Spirit descended upon Him filling Him with power for ministry. We have talked at length about the first three events and touched on the fourth event in the last chapter. Now I want to bring the baptism with the Holy Spirit into a biblical focus because the Gospel of Jesus Christ is more than simply being forgiven, cleansed, and brought into a new family—the Gospel is also the power to live and serve in this world as Jesus Himself did.

Doctrine of Baptisms

Though we have studied and applied the power that God offers us through the important symbol of baptism, the Bible talks about distinct baptisms. Hebrews 6:1-2 says,

Therefore, leaving the discussion of the elementary principles of Christ, let us go on to perfection, not laying again the foundation of repentance from dead works and of faith toward

*God, of **the doctrine of baptisms**, of laying on of hands, of resurrection of the dead, and of eternal judgment.*

Note the plurality of *baptisms*—there is more than one baptism. When we baptize, Jesus told us to do so in the name of the *Father,* and in the name of the *Son,* and in the name of the *Holy Spirit.* Even the verbiage is rather significant. As we take people under the water we say something like, "I baptize you in the name of the Father, Son, and Holy Spirit." Now, there is nothing wrong with saying this, yet this is not what Jesus was saying; that we simply put someone in the water reciting the three names. In using each of the three names separately (...*and* in the name of...), He is designating each as a different baptism: The Baptism of the Father. The Baptism of the Son. And the Baptism of the Holy Spirit.

We have already dealt with two of them extensively. Yet each of these baptisms is distinct one from another and every disciple of Jesus Christ must respond to each of these three baptisms.[22]

The Baptism of the Holy Spirit

This first baptism is the Baptism **of** the Holy Spirit (not to be confused with baptism **in** or **with** the Holy Spirit). It is the baptism of the Holy Spirit because it is He who does the baptizing, and He baptizes us **into the Father**—the family of God. This is when we are saved and are adopted into the family and God and He becomes our Father. 1 Corinthians 12:13 makes it plain, *"For by one Spirit we were all baptized into one body...and have all been made to drink into one Spirit."* In order to enter into God's freedom and family, we must be forgiven of our sins. This is a work of the Holy Spirit that unites us to Christ and the family of God. Further, it is the Holy Spirit who helps us to even be able to call out to God as our Father (Romans 8:15; Galatians 4:6).

Also, 1 Corinthians 12:3 tells us that without the Holy Spirit, we cannot even declare that Jesus Christ is Lord. 1 Peter 3:18 tells us, *"For Christ also suffered once for sins, the just for the unjust, that He might bring us to God, being put to death in the flesh but made alive by the Spirit."* As Jesus died, so did we with Him; we who were *"dead in our trespasses and sins,"* (Ephesians 2:1), He made alive by the same Spirit. In fact, Romans 8:11 says that the same Spirit who raised Jesus from the dead lives in us! This is the regenerating Spirit of life that brings us back from spiritual death the moment we believe on Jesus Christ.

The Baptism of the Father

The second baptism is of the Father. The Father does the baptizing, and He baptizes us **into** the Son, Jesus Christ. As we have seen, through baptism in water we are submitting to God's work and He unites us to Jesus' death and resurrection. It is the symbol of our salvation and repentance; the cleansing of our conscience; and the transformation of our being. If this isn't being baptized into Jesus, I don't know what is! Hebrews 2:11 alludes to the fact that Jesus is our brother. He is not our Father, but we have the **same** Father (John 20:17), and as His children, the Father unites us together so we live as His family **in Christ.**

From the founding of the nation of Israel, God gave the pattern for the complete Gospel in Christ Jesus that we should follow. It is interesting to note how God instructed Moses to build the Tabernacle on Mt. Sinai. God gave specific instructions for its construction. All of the various pieces of furniture of the Tabernacle represent Jesus Christ and God's plan that would be completed through Him. Though the entire Tabernacle is a worthy study, for our purposes we will only look at the outside of the Tabernacle.

A curtain surrounded the entire Tabernacle compound, and there was only one entry point. In John 10:9, Jesus declared, *"I am the door."* Moreover in John 14:6 Jesus also said, *"I am the way and the truth and the life. No one comes to the Father except through Me."* There is only one door that leads to God, and that is through Jesus. Contrary to the popular thought of our world today, not every religion leads to the same place. God is clear—only through His Son, Jesus Christ, can we find the road that leads to God's presence and eternal life.

As the priest walked through that one door into the Tabernacle compound, in front of him was the Bronze Altar—the place where the people would bring their sacrifices for their sins. Every sacrifice offered upon that Altar was a representation of the ultimate sacrifice that Jesus would make on the cross for the world—the place where His blood was shed so that we could be forgiven. It is symbolic of the first Passover where all who were "under the blood" were spared death. This event represents the first baptism of being forgiven of sin so we can be in relationship with God again and part of His family.

In the courtyard of the Tabernacle, beyond the Bronze Altar, stood the Laver, or the washbasin. As we saw in earlier, the Laver is the symbol of the second baptism in water. In the first baptism that the Holy Spirit gives to unite us to the family of God in salvation, we are freed from sin, but the second represents our repentance for sins and the submission of our lives to God. In other words, before the Israelite priest could enter into the Tabernacle and the Holy Place, he first had to go through the process of forgiveness and cleansing. It is no different with us. We are both forgiven through the blood of Christ, and cleansed from our past way of living through the washing of water (see Ezekiel 36:25 and Ephesians 5:26 in reference to the Church). However, before entering the Tabernacle, there was still one more thing for the priests to do— they had to be anointed with oil. This oil represents the third baptism.

The Baptism of the Son

John the Baptist said Jesus would baptize us with the

Holy Spirit and with fire (Matthew 3:11), and Jesus said that when He went away, He would send the Holy Spirit (John 14:16). This is the Baptism *of* the Son— also known as the Baptism *in* or ***with*** the Holy Spirit. Jesus is who does the baptizing into the Holy Spirit!

We need to see the amazing symbolism, power, tenderness, and high calling of these three baptisms. Jesus prayed in John 17 that we would be one with Him and the Father just as He and the Father are one—we were created to be fully united with the Trinity. God so longs for us to be fully united to Him that each member of the Trinity baptizes us into the others with a specific baptism so Jesus' prayer might be fulfilled,

"I pray that they will all be one, just as you and I are one—as you are in me, Father, and I am in you. And may they be in us so that the world will believe you sent me. I have given them the glory you gave me, so they may be one as we are one. I am in them and you are in me. May they experience such perfect unity that the world will know that you sent me and that you love them as much as you love me…I have revealed you to them, and I will continue to do so. Then your love for me will be in them, and I will be in them." *(John 17:21-23; 26)*

The Baptism with the Holy Spirit

Jesus received this baptism with the Holy Spirit when the Spirit descended upon Him in the form of a dove. This occurred at the same time He was baptized in water. This baptism ignited God's supernatural power for Jesus to live and minister. In fact, it is essential to note that Jesus did not minister to people, perform miracles, or preach before He received the Holy Spirit.

It is immensely important to recognize both the divinity and the humanity of Jesus. Many people think that Jesus had miracle-working power because of His divinity. Philippians 2:7 tells us that *"[Jesus] made Himself of no reputation, taking the form of a bondservant, and coming in the likeness of men."* In other words, though He was God, He did not draw from His own divinity to function in divine power. He lived the same as you and I do—as a simple human being. So how could He do so many miraculous works if He did not use His divinity? It is because He was filled with God's Holy Spirit. For this reason, He was able to say to His disciples that *"He who believes in Me, the works I do he will also do, and even greater works...because I go to My Father"* (John 14:12).

Jesus went to the Father so He could send to us who believe, the same Holy Spirit that empowered Him! (See John 14:26 and Acts 1:4). Jesus, though never forsaking His divinity or His position in the God-head, functioned in the Spirit as you and I do—as humans. His empowerment flowed not from His divinity, but from being filled with the power of the Holy Spirit. You and I can receive the same empowerment of the Holy Spirit in our lives to function as Jesus did—this is the third baptism!

Returning to the imagery of the Tabernacle, the High Priest had to pass through the door, the Bronze Altar, the Laver, and before entering the Holy Place where God's presence would be encountered, he had to receive the oil of anointing. What an image of the Holy Spirit! Throughout Scripture, one of the most frequent reflections of the work of the Holy Spirit is oil. The imagery of the Tabernacle reflects the complete Gospel. In the life and ministry of Jesus, this Gospel is realized and made available to us. In the times of the Tabernacle, only a priest could come near God's presence, but in Jesus, the way is open so that all can share in the totality of His power, love, and Kingdom.

The Three Baptisms In Scripture

It is evident that the Baptism with the Holy Spirit is an experience that happens after salvation, and many times after water baptism, but not exclusively after water baptism. Through Scripture, we see the fulfillment of the Holy Spirit even beyond the Tabernacle imagery. 1 Corinthians 10:2, referencing the Israelites as they were leaving Egypt, explains that they *"all were baptized into Moses in the cloud and in the sea."* The Israelites' baptism was in the cloud (the glory cloud of God: the Holy Spirit), in the sea (the waters of baptism), and in Moses (who was a type of Christ-Savior). The Apostle John continues instructing us about these three baptisms:

This is He who came by water and blood—

Jesus Christ; not only by water, but by water and blood. And it is the Spirit who bears witness, because the Spirit is truth. For there are three that bear witness in heaven: the Father, the Word, and the Holy Spirit; and these three are one. And there are three that bear witness on earth: the Spirit, the water, and the blood; and these three agree as one. (1 John 5:6-8)

Consider that fact that the Apostle John presents **three** that give testimony in the earth as well as in heaven: the blood, the water, and the Spirit. The blood represents the work of Jesus in salvation, the water represents baptism, and the Spirit represents power of the Holy Spirit. I also find it fascinating that when Jesus gave the Great Commission, He told His disciples to make disciples of all nations baptizing them in the Name of the 1) Father, and of the 2) Son, and of the, 3) Holy Spirit! The nature of baptism, as we have discussed, is entrance into an abundant and full life that is available to us through the Godhead. We are baptized into the scope of influence, power, and life that each member of the Trinity disposes to us.[23]

Scripture makes it clear that a type of baptism must be received in each of these names. Acts 8:14-16 shows us these different baptisms:

Now when the apostles who were at Jerusalem heard that Samaria had received the word of

God, they sent Peter and John to them, who,
when they had come down, prayed for them
that they might receive the Holy Spirit. For as
yet He had fallen upon none of them. <u>They had</u>
<u>only been baptized in the name of the Lord</u>
<u>Jesus.</u>

In other words, there was forgiveness of sins and belief
in the Savior, but there was not yet full entrance into
the **complete** life God has for His people through the
baptism in the Holy Spirit. Acts gives a further account
of these different baptisms in 10:44-48. The Apostle
Peter is preaching to Cornelius and his household who
were the first Gentiles to believe:

While Peter was still speaking these words, the
Holy Spirit fell upon all those who heard the
word. And those of the circumcision who
believed were astonished, as many as came
with Peter, because the gift of the Holy Spirit
had been poured out on the Gentiles also. For
they heard them speak with tongues and
magnify God. Then Peter answered, "Can
anyone forbid water, that these should not be
baptized who have received the Holy Spirit just
as we have?" <u>And he commanded them to be</u>
<u>baptized in the name of the Lord</u>...

These Gentiles were baptized in the Holy Spirit before
they were baptized in the Name of Jesus, yet Peter
deems it a necessity to be baptized in Jesus' Name, not

just in the Holy Spirit. See again in Acts 19:1-6 what the Apostle Paul does when he finds that believers in Corinth had only repented of their sins:

And it happened, while Apollos was at Corinth, that Paul, having passed through the upper regions, came to Ephesus. And finding some disciples he said to them, "Did you receive the Holy Spirit when you believed?" So they said to him, "We have not so much as heard whether there is a Holy Spirit." And he said to them, "Into what then were you baptized?" So they said, "Into John's baptism."
Then Paul said, "John indeed baptized with a baptism of repentance, saying to the people that they should believe on Him who would come after him, that is, on Christ Jesus."
When they heard this, <u>they were baptized in the name of the Lord Jesus</u>. And when Paul had laid hands on them<u>, the Holy Spirit came upon them</u>, and they spoke with tongues and prophesied.

Before the ascension of Christ into Heaven, Jesus told His disciples not to go anywhere until they had received the Holy Spirit for the same reason that He Himself did not minister before receiving the same Spirit—there was no power! (Acts 1:4-5). The order to wait was accompanied with the promise of power:
"...But you shall receive power when the Holy Spirit has come upon you; and you shall be witnesses to Me

in Jerusalem, and in all Judea and Samaria, and to
the end of the earth" (Acts 1:8). When the Holy Spirit
was poured out upon them, the Church was born and
they began to speak in other tongues, heal the sick and
preach the Gospel. In short, baptism in the Name and
the power of the Holy Spirit was never viewed as
optional by Jesus or the Apostles. Wherever they went,
baptism in the Holy Spirit accompanied baptism in the
Name of Jesus.

Receiving The Holy Spirit

All three baptisms are available for us right now. If you
have never received Jesus as your Lord and Savior, you
can do it right now! Simply ask Him to forgive you of
your sins, confess that He is Lord, and believe that He
died on the cross and that God raised Him from the
dead (Romans 10:9-10). If you have never been
baptized in water, do it! As the Ethiopian, who, having
just believed in Christ, said to Philip, *"Here is water.
What hinders me from being baptized?"* (Acts 8:36).
Nothing hinders you!

In the same way, the baptism with the Holy Spirit is
available to you. As a matter of fact, it is the promise of
the Father! You receive it in the same way you received
salvation—by faith. In Luke 11:9-13, Jesus encourages
His followers to ask for the Holy Spirit:

*So I say to you, ask, and it will be given to you;
seek, and you will find; knock, and it will be
opened to you. For everyone who asks receives,*

and he who seeks finds, and to him who knocks it will be opened. If a son asks for bread from any father among you, will he give him a stone? Or if he asks for a fish, will he give him a serpent instead of a fish? Or if he asks for an egg, will he offer him a scorpion? If you then, being evil, know how to give good gifts to your children, how much more will your heavenly Father give the **Holy Spirit** *to those who ask Him!*

Receiving the baptism of the Holy Spirit is an experience every bit as supernatural as when Jesus forgave you of your sins and redeemed your life. Many people are tentative when they come to receiving the baptism of the Holy Spirit. Much of the hesitancy comes from either **misunderstanding** of the nature of the baptism with the Holy Spirit, or from **abuses** and bizarre practices they have observed from well-intentioned, but spiritually immature people.

We are exhorted in 1 Corinthians 12:1 to not "be ignorant" of the gifts of the Holy Spirit. We should be both familiar with the gifts and mature in our ability to use them, and to be Scripturally grounded with both their functions and their reason for existing.

The list of the gifts of the Holy Spirit are detailed in 1 Corinthians 12: 8-10: the Word of Wisdom, the Word of Knowledge, Faith, Gifts of Healing, Miracles, Prophecy, Discernment of Spirits, Tongues, and Interpretation of

Tongues. Without going into a detailed teaching, their functions are power to free people from the devil's oppression, engage in vital spiritual warfare, and engage in deeper, more fulfilling worship through the Holy Spirit's help.[24] A mentor of mine once told me that there are four categories of the gifts of the Holy Spirit are given to us to help us: 1) to **do** things that we could not do without His help. 2) To **say** things that we could not say with out His help. 3) To **know** things that we could not know without His help. And 4) to **be** the people we could not be without His help. But the ultimate reason for their existence and the manner in which they are to be implemented is explained in 1 Corinthians 13: Love—the sacrificial love that works for the best in one another. When the mature believer understands these things, there will never be a reason to fear the moving or manifestations that the Holy Spirit gives to His people.

Receiving the baptism with the Holy Spirit is to simply open yourself up to the fullness of the promise of the Father. Ask Jesus to baptize you, and receive it with faith. The most common expression of the baptism with the Holy Spirit is speaking in tongues, but it is not wise to adhere to dogma that declares this is the **only** way God can initially express Himself in the life of the believer. However, throughout the book of Acts, and in the experience of many ministers, speaking in tongues is the most common initial expression of the Holy Spirit's filling.

I want to invite you to ask the Holy Spirit to fill you with power to live to the maximum of what God intended for you. You will see that when you receive these three baptisms, your life will never be the same. You will be living the power of Heaven here on earth! That is not to say that everything will automatically become easy, but that the realities of life in Jesus and all of heaven's resources are available to live a victorious life. Neither baptism into the family of God, in water, or in the Holy Spirit, are steps that come and go in a moment. Each is a doorway, that when opened, brings us into a new world and a new way of living in God's grace and power. God is inviting all of us to live every day in the power of baptism.

Addendum: Infant Baptism

If you are reading this short book, it is very possible that your parents had you baptized as an infant or a young child. If that is the case, what a beautiful thing your parents did for you! It is a testimony to their desire that you would walk in obedience in the ways of God. Child baptism is much like a dedication to God. A dedication and an infant baptism are not for the eternal salvation of a person.

Salvation does not come through a ritual, but rather through personal faith in Jesus Christ and the sincerity of repentant hearts for the sin that was committed. It is only through the death and resurrection of Jesus Christ that we can have salvation and remission of our sins. In fact, this is the symbolic meaning of water baptism. Being baptized as an adult and making your own decision to follow Jesus, even though you may have been baptized as a child, is not at all inconsistent with the baptism that your parents provided for you. Rather, it would be more of a fulfillment of the step of dedication and faith your parents took. Their desire that you would walk in God's ways all the days of your life is, in effect, being fulfilled by your willing participation in the death and resurrection of Jesus in the waters of baptism.

The dedication of children to the Lord is actually very biblical. Luke 2:22 teaches, *"Now when the days of her purification according to the law of Moses were completed, they brought Him [Jesus] to Jerusalem to present Him to the Lord."* Although we do not practice the baptizing of infants and small children in our tradition, we do *dedicate* them to the Lord. Children are precious to the Lord and to us as well. We desire that each comes to know Jesus Christ as their personal Lord and Savior, and this is a decision of faith that each person must come to and no one else can make for them. But as parents, we can present our children to the Lord in **recognition** of the gift that God has given to us in our children and the **responsibility** we have in raising them according His ways. You are invited to come and be baptized, not with a sense of obligation or duty, but of one being called by the Lord and taking a willing step to enter into a new dimension of spiritual life and vitality.

Appendix

CHAPTER 3

1. Augustine, *On Christian Doctrine*, II:1

2. St. Augustine: *Letters* 98:2 [A.D. 408]

3. Hawthorne, Gerald, Martin, Ralph P., Reid, Daniel G. *Dictionary of Paul and His Letters*, (Downers Grove, IVP, 1993), 62

CHAPTER 4

4. Thomas, R. L. (1998). *New American Standard Hebrew-Aramaic and Greek dictionaries : updated edition.* (Anaheim: Foundation Publications, Inc.)

5. Allegory taken from Jack Hayford's series *Honest to God*, (SC122CD), Jack Hayford Ministries, Southlake, TX.

6. Keener, Craig. (2003). Gilgal. In (C. Brand, C. Draper, A. England, S. Bond, E. R. Clendenen, & T. C. Butler, Eds.) *Holman Illustrated Bible Dictionary.* (Nashville, TN: Holman Bible Publishers.)

7. Huntzinger, Jon. Lecture given at The King's University for the class: Introduction to the New Testament, 2008

8. Brown, Colin. *Dictionary of New Testament Theology, vol. 1,* (Grand Rapids, Zondervan, 1975), 144

9. Kittle, Gerhardt. *Theological Dictionary of the New Testament, volume 1* (Grand Rapids, Eerdmans Publishing Company, 1964, reprinted 1999), 530

10. Lewis, C. S. (2009-05-28). Mere Christianity (C.S. Lewis Signature Classics) (pp. 196-197). HarperCollins. Kindle Edition.

CHAPTER 5

11. Kittle, Gerhardt. *Theological Dictionary of the New Testament, volume 4* (Grand Rapids, Eerdmans Publishing Company, 1964, reprinted 1999), 946

12. Swanson, J. (1997). Dictionary of Biblical Languages with Semantic Domains : Hebrew (Old Testament). Oak Harbor: Logos Research Systems, Inc.

13. Kittle, Gerhardt. *Theological Dictionary of the New Testament, volume 1* (Grand Rapids,

Eerdmans Publishing Company, 1964, reprinted 1999), 534

CHAPTER 6

14. Baker, Tom. *Incarnation.* (College Station, TX: Virtualbookworm.com Publishing Inc.), 7

15. Lewis, C. S. Mere Christianity (C.S. Lewis Signature Classics) (p. 178). HarperCollins. Kindle Edition.

16. Lewis, C. S. (2009-05-28). Mere Christianity (C.S. Lewis Signature Classics) (p. 92). HarperCollins. Kindle Edition.

17. Lewis, C. S. (2009-05-28). Mere Christianity (C.S. Lewis Signature Classics) (pp. 191-192). HarperCollins. Kindle Edition.

CHAPTER 7

18. Mannoia, Kevin and Thorsen, Don. The Holiness Manifesto, (Eerdmans: Grand Rapids, 2008), 30-31, article by Jonathan Huntzinger

19. Ross, A. P. *Genesis.* In J. F. Walvoord & R. B. Zuck (Eds.), *The Bible Knowledge Commentary: An Exposition of the* (Wheaton, IL: Victor Books, 1985), 30

20. Huntzinger, Jon. Lecture given at The King's University for the class: New Testament Survey, 2008

21. Peterson, Eugene H. (2011-03-11). The Message Numbered Edition Hardback (Kindle Locations 60370-60373). Navpress. Kindle Edition.

CHAPTER 8

22. Hayford, Jack. *Newborn*, (Wheaton, IL, Tyndale House Publishing, 1987), 61

23. Hayford, Jack, Lecture at The King's University, March 2015

24. Hayford, Jack W. *Spirit-Filled: Anointed by Christ the King* (Van Nuys, CA, Living Way Ministries, 1984)

About the Author

Kyle W. Bauer has a rich ministry history spanning more than a decade. Grandson of iconic Foursquare pastor, Jack W. Hayford, Kyle has distinguished himself as a pastor and leader in his own right. Throughout his career, he's served as a children's pastor, a church planter, a missionary in Mexico, and a professor of ministry and history at the King's University. His current ministry assignment is serving as pastor at La Iglesia En El Camino Santa Clarita, in Santa Clarita, California. Kyle holds a Bachelor's Degree in Theological Studies and a Master's Degree in Divinity, both from The King's University. He and his wife, Teresa, were married in 2003 and have four children—three boys, and one girl.

For more information or to contact Kyle, you can visit his site www.kwbauer.com

This book is available in English and Spanish at www.amazon.com

Made in United States
North Haven, CT
03 June 2022